Editor's Note on Growth Framework for Cannapreneurs: Immutable Tenets for Unrivaled Market Success

Prepared by Adam Anderson, a co-founder of Cooler Collaborative LLC, a leading Denver-based cannabis marketing and consulting firm, **Growth Framework for Cannapreneurs**: *Immutable Tenets for Unrivaled Market Success* is more than just a book; it's a beacon for those venturing into the burgeoning cannabis industry in the USA. Drawing from deep industry insights and a wealth of experience, this book is meticulously crafted to fortify cannabis enterprises, propelling them towards unparalleled success in an ever-evolving market landscape. Dive in to unlock a wealth of knowledge from the epicenter of cannabis entrepreneurship.

Website: www.coolercollaborative.com
Email: inquiry@coolercollaborative.com
Contact: (407) 536-7474

 **1.5 million jobs.** The cannabis industry is estimated to create over 1.5 million jobs in the US by 2025. New Frontier Data.

 **18 States.** US number of states that have legalized cannabis for recreational use. Wikipedia. 65% of US cannabis sales that are generated by medical sales.

 Approximately half of Americans, some 78 million people, claimed to have used marijuana at some point in their lifetime

 Cannabis legalization has generated over $20 billion in tax revenue for state and local governments since 2014.

Table of Contents

Preface	1
Select Your Octane	2
Know Your History	5
Embrace Opportunity	13
Arrive at Aha!	15
Know Thy Customer	17
Make Data Your King	23
Stand Out	27
Elevate Your Brand	31
Refine Your Offerings	38
Streamline Your Ops	44
Embrace Technology	50
Post for Impact	56
Create Content	62
Master Your Mix	66
Automate Everything	71
Be Active in Activating	80
Befriend Exposure	92
Schedule A Discovery	97
Conclusion	98

Preface

By **Adam Anderson**, Strategic Architect in Business Growth

The cannabis industry's ascendancy is unparalleled in modern commerce, seamlessly transitioning from obscurity to mainstream prominence. At its core, cannabis embodies transformation, resilience, and the essence of the entrepreneurial spirit. Succeeding here is more than industry participation—it's about shaping its evolution and championing change.

Throughout my career, I've discerned universal markers of entrepreneurial success and familiar pitfalls. However, cannabis presents a singular challenge—a symphony of traditional wisdom and emerging innovations, played against a backdrop of evolving regulations and shifting consumer dynamics.

This tome distills a lifetime of expertise into crucial domains indispensable for the modern cannabis entrepreneur. Each tenet is a pillar, providing stability and direction to those aiming to plant their flag in this burgeoning sector. Delve into the regulatory intricacies, harness the pulse of consumer trends, leverage avant-garde technologies, and become a masterful cannabis raconteur.

While these guiding tenets lay a solid foundation, remember the cannabis arena's inherent fluidity. Today's trend can be tomorrow's relic. But with this foundational knowledge, you're primed to pivot, innovate, and lead.

Embracing the Cannapreneurship journey is about laying down a legacy in the expanse of this industry. Let this work illuminate your path, guiding your voyage through the multifaceted cannabis odyssey.

In a dynamic business realm, mere survival is passe; visionary leadership is the key. Armed with insights from this guide, you're not just prepared for the present—you're future-proofed, ready to craft a lasting legacy amidst the ebbs and flows of an unpredictable market.

To enduring growth and boundless green possibilities,

Adam Anderson

Adam Anderson, Co-founder
Cooler Collaborative LLC.

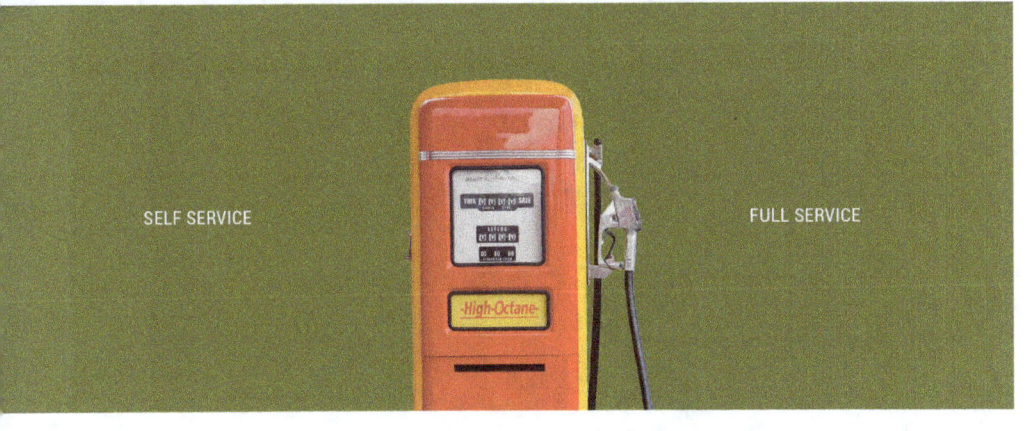

SELF SERVICE

FULL SERVICE

Select Your Octane

As you chart your journey in the cannabis business, two distinct options lay before you: the self-service growth mode and the full-service growth partnership. Are you a self-starter? Then **Self-Service Growth Mode** is tailored for you, offering an A-Z guide from foundational elements to scaling strategies. Expect a bounty of rich insights, methodical instructions, and practical worksheets—each informed by years of experience in guiding global brands toward accelerated growth.

If you're inclined to seek expert collaboration, the **Full Service Growth Partnership** is your ticket. Skip ahead to the "Discovery" chapter to begin a specialized collaboration with Cooler Collaborate's Business Growth Team. Simply fill out the forms, and what you'll get back is far more than mere analysis; it's your business's future mapped out. We'll carve out a custom growth strategy just for you, transforming your aspirations into reachable milestones.

So, whether you opt for self-guidance or expert-led growth, know this: Cooler Collaborate's Business Growth Team stands ready to amplify your success. Dive into the option that speaks to you, and when you're ready for that transformational leap, rest assured, we're here to join forces with you.

Self-Service Growth

Here are eight compelling benefits distilled from reading Growth Framework for Cannapreneurs:

- **Master Your Brand:** Elevate your cannabis brand's presence and positioning, ensuring it resonates with your ideal customers.

- **Strategic Growth:** Craft and implement a comprehensive growth plan meticulously tailored to the cannabis industry's unique challenges.

- **Digital Domination:** Boost online visibility through expert SEO strategies, PPC campaigns, and an impactful digital footprint, setting you apart in a saturated market.

- **Engage & Convert:** Leverage cutting-edge social media and email marketing techniques to captivate your audience, nurture leads, and transform them into loyal customers.

- **Operational Excellence:** Streamline operations, from product rollout to CRM systems, ensuring seamless customer experiences and efficient business processes.

- **Measure and Pivot:** Monitor key performance indicators with precision, making informed decisions to constantly refine your market strategy for unparalleled success.

- **Forge Powerful Partnerships:** Harness the potential of affiliate and partnership marketing, tapping into wider audiences and synergistic collaborations to amplify your cannabis brand's reach and influence.

- **Innovative Inbound Techniques:** Learn how to magnetically attract potential customers to your business through content and experiences specially tailored for the cannabis market, ensuring genuine engagement and higher conversions.

Armed with these insights, cannabis entrepreneurs can chart a path to market dominance!

Full-Service Growth Partnership

1. Discovery Session:

   - Duration: 1-2 hours
   - Purpose: Understand your business vision, challenges, and goals.

2. Comprehensive Growth Metrics Assessment:

   - Brand: Analyze brand identity, consistency, and recall.
   - Market Position: Determine current standing in the cannabis market.
   - Marketing Metrics: Evaluate marketing KPIs and effectiveness.
   - MVP (Minimum Viable Product): Assess product fit in the market.
   - Competition: Understand competitors' strengths and vulnerabilities.
   - Product & Service: Examine the offerings' quality and demand.
   - Operations: Review efficiency and productivity of business processes.
   - Technology: Gauge the aptness and adoption of tech solutions.
   - Social Media: Analyze presence, engagement, and content strategy.
   - Digital Footprint: Measure online visibility and impact.

3. Growth Score Evaluation:

   - Outcome: A quantifiable score indicating your current growth status.

4. Bespoke Growth Plan Development:

   - Detailed, customized plan to meet growth aspirations.
   - Clear growth targets defined to track progress.

5. Collaborative Implementation:

   - Ongoing partnership with the Cooler Collaborative team.
   - Quarterly review meetings to ensure targets are met and to adapt to any market changes.

At Cooler Collaborative, we're committed to your transformational growth journey. With our systematic approach, we'll navigate the growth path together, ensuring your cannabis business not only thrives but excels.

Know Your History

Cannabis in the 1960s: Between Counterculture and the Corridors of Power

The 1960s, with their psychedelic hues, anti-establishment cries, and swirling, smoky dreams, laid down an unmistakable legacy for America. But as the era swirled with change, few symbols captured its essence like cannabis. The delicate leaves of this plant, embraced by rebels and reviled by regulators, would set the stage for a societal tug-of-war spanning decades.

By the time Jimi Hendrix's guitar wailed through Woodstock and peace signs were as ubiquitous as morning coffee, cannabis had firmly rooted itself in the nation's collective consciousness. An estimated 8% of Americans had experienced its allure by 1970, a number that might seem meager today but was revolutionary then. From the anti-war protests to the intimate gatherings in Greenwich Village, cannabis was not just a substance but a statement.

Yet, as history so often illustrates, countercultural movements are met with governmental counteractions. The Controlled Substances Act of 1970 categorized cannabis as a Schedule I drug, placing it alongside substances like heroin. For lawmakers, this was a declaration of danger. For the free spirits of the time, it was an affront. The federal government's message was clear: cannabis, despite its growing cultural capital, was an outlaw.

But to truly appreciate cannabis's iconic status in the 1960s, one must travel back to San Francisco's "Summer of Love" in 1967. The streets of Haight-Ashbury were not merely roads but runways, flaunting an elaborate display of colorful garb, impassioned ideologies, and yes, the unmistakable scent of cannabis. The Summer wasn't just a season but a sentiment. And in this panorama, cannabis was more than a mere indulgence—it was an emblem, a beacon of resistance against convention and control.

The dual identity of cannabis in the 1960s—as both a cherished emblem of counterculture and a contentious point in policymaking—foreshadowed the complex journey ahead. While the decade ended with the substance under legal siege, its spirit, encapsulated in a haze of hope and rebellion, persisted. The seeds, both literal and metaphorical, had been sown, ready to sprout in the subsequent decades of America's evolving relationship with the green muse.

The 1970s: Cannabis at the Crossroads of Change

As the 1960s' kaleidoscopic haze began to settle, the 1970s dawned with an aura of introspection. The nation, coming to terms with the Vietnam War's echoes and the Civil Rights Movement's triumphs, seemed ready to question the established orthodoxy. At

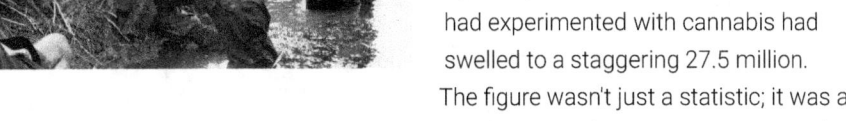

the heart of this burgeoning debate stood cannabis—a plant that had, in the previous decade, become emblematic of rebellion. But the '70s would not be about rebellion; it would be about re-evaluation.

By 1979, the number of Americans who had experimented with cannabis had swelled to a staggering 27.5 million. The figure wasn't just a statistic; it was a statement. From college campuses to clandestine downtown lounges, a joint passed between fingers was also passing the message of change. Cannabis, once the emblem of the radical, had nudged its way into the mainstream.

This shift in public sentiment was beginning to manifest in legislative arenas. Oregon, ever the trailblazer, heralded a new dawn in 1973 when it decriminalized cannabis. Although this did not constitute outright legalization, it was a beginning and offered a glimpse of a time when attitudes toward cannabis might be less fear- and prejudice-based.

Yet, any history of the '70s cannabis movement would be incomplete without nodding to the National Organization for the Reform of Marijuana Laws, or NORML. Founded in 1970, at the decade's very onset, NORML became the clarion voice advocating for cannabis policy changes. More than just a lobby, it epitomized the era's zeitgeist—a collective realization that the time had come to reconsider old stances and stigmas.

In their advocacy, NORML didn't just argue for a plant; they argued for a principle. Their message was clear: In a nation where personal freedom was paramount, the criminalization of cannabis was not just untenable but fundamentally un-American. Their work, built on a foundation of scientific scrutiny, legal acumen, and impassioned activism, underscored the decade's ethos of transformation.

The 1970s, then, stood as a transitional epoch for cannabis. From the shadows of countercultural symbolism, the plant stepped into the limelight of public discourse. As disco beats throbbed in the background and a new world order took shape, cannabis found itself not as a relic of a bygone rebellious age but as a harbinger of a future, one more compassionate, more understanding, and more accepting.

The 1980s: Cannabis in the Trenches of a War

The 1980s, awash in neon hues and synthesizer beats, brought forth a curious paradox. While pop culture icons crooned about freedom and self-expression, behind the gilded curtain, America was gearing up for war. Not against a foreign power, but against a more intimate adversary: drugs. In this fervent climate, cannabis found itself ensnared, a hapless foot soldier in the sprawling battleground of the "War on Drugs."

The governmental machinery, with its seemingly boundless reserves, was quick to move. By 1987, the treasury was bleeding a staggering $1 billion annually on anti-drug campaigns, painting a picture of a nation under siege. Television sets across the country flickered with images of cracked eggs and heated pans, imparting the message, "This is your brain on drugs."

The culmination of this sentiment was encapsulated in the Anti-Drug Abuse Act of 1986, a piece of legislation that wielded punitive measures with an almost evangelical fervor. Under its aegis, drug offenses, including those involving cannabis, attracted steep penalties. For a brief period, it appeared as though an uncompromising storm had taken the place of the gentle haze of the 1960s and the emerging acceptance of the 1970s.

But as history has often shown, strict impositions often give birth to fervent resistance. A notable embodiment of this resistance was the counter-narrative emerging against

programs like D.A.R.E., established in 1983. On the surface, D.A.R.E. presented itself as a benign educational initiative, aiming to steer schoolchildren away from drugs. However, beneath this veneer lies a more complex reality. Many began to view it as the epitome of anti-cannabis propaganda, a clarion call to rally against.

This decade, with its pulsating music and political tumult, became the crucible in which America's relationship with cannabis was tested. The stringent crackdowns did more than just penalize users; they galvanized a generation. Advocates, activists, and everyday citizens began to question, critique, and challenge the status quo. As the '80s drew to a close, it was evident that the War on Drugs had inadvertently sown the seeds for a future revolution, where cannabis would emerge not as a villain but as a symbol of a nation's evolving consciousness.

The 1990s: When Cannabis Turned Clinical

Amidst the grunge music, the flannel shirts, and the rise of the dot-com bubble, the 1990s ushered in a seismic shift in America's perception of cannabis. As the ashes of the War on Drugs began to settle, a new narrative emerged, not from the smoky haze of counterculture basements but from the sterile confines of clinics and medical research facilities.

In 1996, California, ever the harbinger of change, passed Proposition 215. With a stroke of a pen, the Golden State declared cannabis not just permissible but potentially medicinal. This wasn't just a law—it was a revolution. Cannabis, so long vilified, had stepped into the spotlight, not as a recreational indulgence but as a potential panacea.

By 1999, the notion had taken root deeply in the American psyche. A staggering 73% of Americans now endorse the use of medicinal cannabis. For a plant that had been the poster child of societal decay a mere decade earlier, this was nothing short of a renaissance.

However, for those on the ground, this shift wasn't sudden. It had been brewing quietly and determinedly in places like San Francisco's Cannabis Buyers Club. Founded in the early 1990s, this establishment served as more than just a dispensary—it was a sanctuary. At a time when the AIDS epidemic had cast a long, formidable shadow over

the LGBTQ+ community, the Club emerged as a beacon of hope, spotlighting the role of medicinal cannabis in alleviating the debilitating symptoms of the disease.

It was here, amidst the tales of pain, perseverance, and, eventually, relief, that cannabis's transformation from villain to savior was most palpable. The stories were personal, but their implications were universal. They spoke of a plant that offered solace when synthetic drugs faltered, of a natural remedy that, for many, stood between life and the precipice of unbearable pain.

As the decade came to a close, cannabis, with its myriad shades of green, symbolized the multifaceted nature of America's relationship with it: sometimes recreational, sometimes medicinal, but always deeply, intrinsically human. The 1990s, in essence, weren't just about the plant's emergence as a medical marvel but about America's maturation in understanding, accepting, and embracing its potential.

The 2000s: The Quiet Rebellion of States

The dawn of the new millennium carried the familiar hum of technological marvels, the distant chatter of burgeoning social media, and the ubiquitous sounds of flip phones snapping shut. Beneath these audible layers, however, thrummed a more profound resonance—the incremental, yet unmistakable, march of progress in the realm of cannabis.

The broad declarations of a single entity did not define the 2000s; rather, it was the various, yet harmonious chords that various states struck. While federal regulations remained stoic, almost ossified in their approach to cannabis, states began to dance to a different tune, one that echoed the demands and desires of their citizens. By the time 2008 drew its last breath, 13 states, each with its own unique sociopolitical fabric, had come to a consensus: medical cannabis deserved a place in the annals of legitimate therapeutic avenues.

Fore-fronting this quiet rebellion was Colorado, with Amendment 20 in 2000. Beyond merely legalizing medical cannabis, Colorado's declaration was emblematic—it was an acknowledgment of the plant's complex potential and a nod to the importance of evidence over prejudice. The Centennial State's move was neither the first nor the last,

but it was pivotal, solidifying the idea that the future of cannabis lay not in sweeping federal mandates but in localized, grassroots movements.

Yet, the narrative of this decade is incomplete without a tribute to its most vocal advocates. Millions of people's favorite television personality, Montel Williams,

contributed not only his voice but also his personal journey to the cause. After revealing his Multiple Sclerosis diagnosis in 1999, Williams became synonymous with the medicinal cannabis advocacy movement. His story, fraught with the agonies of MS and the solace he found in cannabis, transformed from a personal ordeal to a public testament. Through Williams, many Americans glimpsed the nuanced realities of life

with chronic illness and the tangible relief that cannabis offered.

The 2000s, thus, stand as a testament to the power of collective action and individual narratives. While the federal leviathan remained unmoved, states and individuals carved out spaces of acceptance, understanding, and, most crucially, empathy. The decade did not see the walls of prejudice tumble down, but it certainly witnessed them crack, one state and one story at a time.

The 2010s: From Healing Herb to Recreational Reverie

In the 2010s, while the globe was preoccupied with the antics of a dancing "Gangnam Style" or the tweets of fledgling world leaders, cannabis was undergoing a transformative renaissance. It was a decade when the emerald leaves of the plant rustled their way from sealed medicinal bottles to the laid-back lounges of recreational users, chronicling a broader shift in American consciousness.

This epoch was defined not just by quiet acceptance but by a jubilant embrace. By the decade's end, a whopping 33 states had given a nod to medicinal cannabis. More remarkably, 11 had flung open the gates to recreational usage. From the hushed whispers of the late 20th century to the celebratory clamor of the 2010s, cannabis has come of age.

Two states, in particular, stood tall as the vanguard of this movement: Colorado and Washington. In 2012, they made a proclamation that would reverberate across state lines, championing the cause of recreational cannabis. This wasn't merely an alteration in legal code; it was a cultural paradigm shift, marking the plant's departure from strictly medicinal contexts to a broader societal milieu.

Yet, what sets the 2010s apart is the tale of economic prowess intertwined with this socio-cultural shift. The story of Denver post-2012 is emblematic. Christened the "Green Rush," the city bore witness to a cannabis-driven economic renaissance. Dispensaries sprouted, tourism flourished, and a once-stigmatized industry was now a lucrative, mainstream enterprise. Through Denver's meteoric rise, the nation glimpsed the future—a fusion of commercial ambition and recreational delight.

In retrospect, the 2010s for cannabis were akin to a butterfly's metamorphosis. From the cocoon of medical necessity emerged a creature of vibrant hues, fluttering freely and embraced by society's changing winds. It was a testament to how deeply embedded the plant had become in the American tapestry, no longer just a therapeutic agent but a symbol of recreation, economic potential, and, above all, societal evolution.

The 2020s: From Counter-Culture to Corner Store

The dawn of the 2020s, ensconced in global pandemics and digital revolutions, brought with it an unexpected advocate for solace and wellbeing—cannabis. This decade bore witness to the plant's most audacious act yet: shedding the last remnants of its renegade past and sauntering confidently into the heart of the American mainstream. It was no longer the rebellious teenager of the 60s or the clinical savior of the 90s; cannabis had matured into a sophisticated adult, fluent in the languages of wellness, economy, and policy.

Supporting this assertion was a statistic that would have been unimaginable a few decades ago: By 2021, a staggering 90% of Americans had cast their votes, not in election booths but in their collective psyche, asserting that cannabis, be it for healing or leisure, deserved legal recognition. This wasn't just acceptance; it was a resounding endorsement.

Reflecting this groundswell of public opinion was a legislative milestone that sent ripples across Capitol Hill. The MORE Act, breezing through the House in 2020, set its sights audaciously high—federal decriminalization. Although its fate in the legislative labyrinth was still uncertain, its very existence and the discourse it generated were indicative of the shifting sands of federal sentiment.

Yet, for all the legal and legislative fanfare, the true barometer of change lay on the unassuming shelves of local stores. CBD, a cannabis derivative, began to make

appearances in the most unlikely of places, from the chic boutiques of Manhattan to the rustic general stores of the Deep South. Its popularity transcended political affiliations and geographical boundaries, morphing into a nationwide phenomenon.

Through CBD, conservative Americans were tacitly nodding to the therapeutic potentials of cannabis, even if they weren't lighting up a joint.

The 2020s, thus far, stand as a testament to cannabis's unparalleled journey. From the fringes to the fore, its tale is one of resilience, evolution, and, ultimately, redemption. As the decade unfolds, one thing is clear: cannabis, in all its multifaceted glory, is here to stay, shaping not just individual experiences but the very fabric of American society and policy.

Embrace Opportunity

> Strong reasons make strong actions.

—William Shakespeare

New York's Evolution and Cannabis' Rise

In the heart of ever-evolving New York, 5th Avenue welcomes another change. Here, among legendary brands, MedMen emerges as more than just a dispensary. It stands as a bold statement, signifying the evolution of the cannabis entrepreneur—savvy,

cultured, and perfectly balancing respect for tradition with business sense. Leaders like Adam Bierman, MedMen's co-founder, are presenting cannabis as both an intricate art and a meticulous science.

For MedMen and its peers, cannabis isn't an arbitrary pursuit. It symbolizes wellness, empowerment, and a mission to shift prevailing views on its potential. Such change is widespread. Cannapreneur Quarterly reports that a striking 65% of new cannabis trailblazers hold advanced degrees. They perceive cannabis as an intersection of health, social advocacy, and business passion.

Yet, navigating this sector isn't straightforward. Despite progressive states like Colorado and California pioneering the way, fluctuating state and federal policies complicate the journey. In fact, the Cannabis Regulatory Journal suggests that almost a third of new ventures face legal challenges in their first year.

Changing longstanding views is another Herculean effort. Cannabis leaders today strive to alter perceptions held for decades by promoting community involvement, supporting medical studies, and advocating for openness. Every product and conversation is an opportunity to challenge or reinforce existing beliefs.

In a world where cannabis dining becomes trendy and dispensaries evolve into cultural landmarks, these leaders aren't merely adapting to trends; they're shaping them. Their audience spans from Boomers to Gen Z, all exploring the cannabis spectrum.

Their defining trait is resilience. They adeptly maneuver complex regulations, establish efficient supply chains, and tirelessly work to shift stigmas. As areas like the East Village dim under evening skies, dispensaries open their doors wide, signaling a clear message: The modern era of cannabis is diverse and driven by trailblazers like MedMen.

Challenges in the Cannabis Landscape:

A Regulatory Puzzle: In the U.S., cannabis regulations vary widely. What's seen as progressive in California might be unlawful in Alabama.

Banking Dilemmas: The clash between state legality and federal caution leads many banks to distance themselves from cannabis businesses, affecting their financial operations.

The Licensing Challenge: Earning the right to operate isn't just about paperwork. With limited licenses available, it becomes a competitive arena.

Digital Hurdles: Major online platforms, like Facebook and Google, restrict cannabis promotions, limiting its digital outreach.

Demographic Balance: Cannabis marketing aims to attract adults, ensuring it doesn't inadvertently target a younger audience.

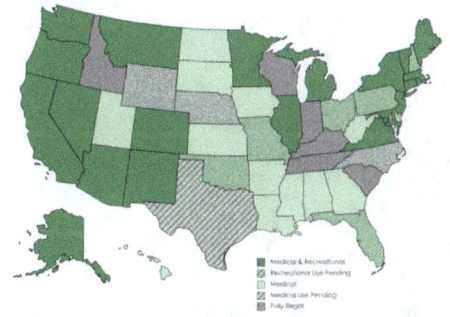

Crafting the Story: Overcoming age-old stereotypes while being cautious around medicinal assertions requires skillful storytelling.

Arrive at Aha!

"

Innovation is taking two things that already exist and putting them together in a new way.

—Tom Freston

Defining moments of clarity are not just inspirational bursts but game-changing events. These "Aha" moments have been pivotal in crafting the narrative of an industry that melds tradition and innovation. This feature delves into how such flashes of insight have, and will continue to, redefine cannabis commerce from the ground up.The Fusion of Tradition and Innovation

The cannabis industry, once steeped in secrecy and cultural significance, is now emerging as a sophisticated market. A glance at any modern cannabis laboratory reveals a dedicated team spending countless hours deciphering legal challenges, understanding market nuances, and experimenting with different strains. The goal? To hit upon that elusive "Aha" moment—a breakthrough that can be as significant as discovering the finest CBD strain or developing a revolutionary marketing tactic. It's a delicate balance between embracing traditional cannabis culture and infusing it with a modern entrepreneurial spirit.

An "Aha" moment is not a mere revelation but a seed of an idea that needs to be nurtured. Just like any agricultural process, it requires the right conditions—resilience, adaptability, and a dash of audacity—to flourish. And this process is not unique to researchers. Entrepreneurs, too, find themselves in the crucible, where an idea, if tended to properly, can yield unprecedented returns. The journey from an idea to execution is fraught with challenges, but it is also one of growth and purpose.

Some of the most transformative "ah-ha" moments come from notable figures who have changed our perspective on cannabis. Dr. Raphael Mechoulam, who first isolated THC in the 1960s, was a pioneer in shedding light on the plant's chemical composition. Then there's Jazmin Hupp, who has carved out a space for female entrepreneurs in the cannabis industry, emphasizing the role of community. Herbert A. Gilbert took innovation a step further by revolutionizing how we consume cannabis by introducing smokeless options.

It's easy to look at these accomplishments as isolated incidents, but they are more than that. Each "aha" moment has the potential to shift the narrative, creating a domino effect of innovation that spans laboratories, grow rooms, and conference halls. They are, in essence, the building blocks that contribute to the industry's collective knowledge and future trajectory.

Every cannabis enthusiast and entrepreneur stands on the brink of contributing to this evolving story. These moments of clarity are not just personal milestones but contribute to the tapestry of an industry in flux. As we look forward, let the insights from industry pioneers serve as both inspiration and guidance. They should be viewed not as an end but as a catalyst, a trigger that sets off a chain of events leading to the next significant moment in cannabis commerce.

The cannabis industry is not just about capitalizing on the moment but about nurturing that moment into something transformative. The "aha" moments, whether experienced by researchers tirelessly decoding the genetic makeup of cannabis or entrepreneurs looking to tap into an unserved niche, have a ripple effect. They redefine the norms and inspire a new wave of thinkers and doers who are crucial for the next chapter in this burgeoning field. Your "aha" moment could very well be the tipping point the industry has been waiting for.

Know Thy Customer

The purpose of business is to create and
keep a customer.

—Peter Drucker

The burgeoning cannabis industry stands as an outlier, striving to weave genuine
human connection into its business fabric. This trend is crystallized in the story of
Jamal and Elena, whose relationship transcends the traditional vendor-customer
dynamic. It's a narrative of empathy and community, a beacon for how the cannabis
industry could set new standards for customer engagement and personalized service.

Picture Elena sipping her morning coffee, listening to podcasts that range from politics
to wellness. Her attention narrows when she hears Jamal, the entrepreneurial spirit
behind 'Emerald Elixirs,' discussing the nuanced benefits of cannabis for chronic pain—
something Elena knows all too well. The podcast isn't just an ad; it's educational, with
an accompanying blog post that dispels common myths about cannabis. This first
touchpoint, a blend of education and sincerity, is the cornerstone of Jamal's customer
engagement strategy.

In Jamal's dispensary, you'll meet people from all walks of life: Rebecca, a war veteran
seeking to manage her PTSD; David, a 40-something parent looking for stress relief;
Maria, a college athlete aiming to improve her recovery routine. The point? Jamal
knows each by name and story, not just by sales metrics. With a staggering 70% higher
customer retention rate, 'Emerald Elixirs' serves as a microcosm of the industry's
paradigm shift toward genuine, long-lasting relationships.

Consider Elena's Journey

Awareness: A podcast serves as the gateway to Elena's engagement with 'Emerald Elixirs.'

Consideration: Elena delves into Jamal's detailed strain reviews and watches an insightful video about the dispensary's customer support policies.

Conversion: A personalized pop-up message from Jamal himself, sharing his vision and values, finally prompts Elena to click the 'Purchase' button.

Retention: Through targeted emails, Jamal introduces Elena to the 'Emerald Loyals' program, cementing her as a recurring customer.

Advocacy: Elena becomes a vocal advocate, sharing her positive experiences through social media, thereby attracting more customers like her to Jamal's store.

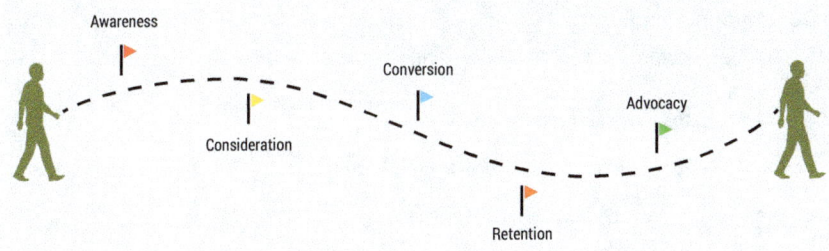

Jamal's understanding of his customers doesn't stem solely from data; he creates intricate 'customer personas.' For example, "Chronic Pain Peter" is in his mid-50s, has suffered from back pain for years, and prefers Indica strains for their soothing effects. Then there's "Yoga Enthusiast Yasmine," who prefers Sativa strains for their energizing effects to augment her practice. These aren't just numbers or demographics; they're layered, human profiles that guide Jamal in offering tailored experiences.

Jamal's enduring relationships with Elena, Peter, Yasmine, and others are not one-sided; they also enhance his business agility. Whether fine-tuning his product range or crafting targeted marketing messages, Jamal's rich understanding of his customer base propels his business to continually evolve and meet distinct needs.

As the cannabis industry gains mainstream acceptance, its inherent power lies in its capacity for human connection. The case of Jamal and Elena underscores how each purchase is not just an economic transaction but a chapter in a rich, evolving narrative. Through meaningful engagement and a deep understanding of each customer's journey, the cannabis industry has a unique opportunity: to set new precedents in how business is not just conducted, but how it is felt. After all, the most valuable capital in any industry is not merely financial; it's profoundly and uniquely human.

What if you could merge analytics with empathy to create a blueprint for customer engagement? Enter the Customer Persona Canvas—a dynamic tool that goes beyond demographic checkboxes to provide a 360-degree view of your consumer, tailored for nuanced and effective marketing. This comprehensive canvas takes you through each element to cultivate real human connections refining the customer experience, boosting brand loyalty, and elevating profitability. Say goodbye to one-size-fits-all strategies; it's time to craft your business approach with the precision of an artist and the insight of a psychologist. Here are the steps you can follow:

1. Setting the Stage

Begin with a template or a blank document. Visualize it as a canvas waiting to be adorned with details.that will breathe life into your imagined consumer.

2. The Demographic Profile
Much like the base layer of a painting, start with broad strokes.

- Name: Give your persona a fictional name to humanize the data.
- Age: A range or specific age that encapsulates your target
- Location: urban loft? Countryside retreat? Pinpoint their locale.
- Occupation: What do they do? Maybe 'John' is a software engineer or 'Alex' is a yoga instructor.
- Income Level: This will influence purchasing decisions.

3. Psychological Layers
Now, venture beneath the surface, capturing the finer nuances:

- Goals and Motivations: Why might 'John' seek cannabis solutions? Stress relief, perhaps?
- Challenges and Pain Points: What barriers does 'John' face in finding the perfect strain?
- Interests and Hobbies: Does 'John' enjoy tranquil hikes or is 'Alex' partial to meditation?

4. The Cannabis Specifics
The essence of your canvas:

- Cannabis Usage: Is it medicinal, recreational, or a blend of both?
- Preferred Strains: Sativa for Energy or Indica for Relaxation?
- Consumption Methods: Edibles, tinctures, vapes, or the old-fashioned way?
- Purchase Frequency: Weekly, monthly, or sporadically?

5. Brand Interactions

- Engagement Channels: Does 'John' discover new strains on Instagram? Or is 'Riley' an email subscriber?

- Feedback Channels: How do they voice their praise or concerns? Reviews, direct messages, or testimonials?

- Purchase Journey: Do they start with online research and then visit a store? Or vice versa?

6. Completing the Picture

Attach a stock photo or an illustration to your persona. This visual cue amplifies the human connection, allowing you and your team to truly "see" your customer.

7. Sources of Inspiration

When crafting your customer persona, focus on real, hard data to bring 'John' or 'Riley' to life. Customer surveys, feedback, reviews, and sales patterns aren't just numbers or random comments; they're the breadcrumbs that lead to a fuller understanding of your customer. Creating this persona is more than just a business exercise—it's a voyage into the very stories that make your market tick. Remember, behind every purchase, every click, and every query lies a human narrative. Grasping that narrative isn't merely a route to success in the cannabis industry; it's your pathway to forging authentic human connections in a market ripe with untapped potential.

John Williams

Background & Demographics
Job? Career path? Family? Lifestyle?
Spending habits? Age? Income? Location?
Gender identity?

Age:

Location:

Gender:

Education:

Profession:

Location:

Lifestyle:

Technology/Social Media
Device preferences? Social media
platforms? Tech savvy?

- Your text here
- Your text here
- Your text here
- Your text here
- Your text here
- Your text here

Goals/Metrics/Motivations
Primary/secondary goals? Personal vs
professional goals? Top metrics they
track? Motivations?

- Your text here
- Your text here
- Your text here
- Your text here
- Your text here
- Your text here

Personality Traits
Introvert vs extrovert? Interested in trying
new things or likes consistency and brands
they trust?

- Your text here
- Your text here
- Your text here
- Your text here
- Your text here
- Your text here

Challenges
What does this person struggle with in
relation to meeting goals? What serves as
a roadblock for this person's success?

- Your text here
- Your text here
- Your text here
- Your text here
- Your text here
- Your text here

John
Williams

Real Quotes
About goals, challenges, etc.

- Your text here
- Your text here
- Your text here
- Your text here
- Your text here
- Your text here

Common Objections
Why wouldn't they buy your product/ service?

- Your text here
- Your text here
- Your text here
- Your text here
- Your text here
- Your text here

What can we do?
...to help our persona achieve their goals? ...to help our persona overcome their challenges?

- Your text here
- Your text here
- Your text here
- Your text here
- Your text here
- Your text here

Marketing Messaging
How can you describe your solution to have the biggest impact on your persona? What resonates most with your persona?

- Your text here
- Your text here
- Your text here
- Your text here
- Your text here
- Your text here

Elevator Pitch/Bumper Sticker
Sell your persona on your solution - in a sentence or a few words!

- Your text here
- Your text here
- Your text here
- Your text here
- Your text here
- Your text here

Page 2 of 2

Note: High-resolution PDF versions of all worksheets and growth canvas templates are available for download at www.coolercollaborative.com.

Make Data Your King

"

In the green tapestry of cannabis
commerce, data is the thread, technology
is the loom, and cultural connection is the
artist's hand.

—Adam Anderson

So, here you are, a cannabis maven standing on the cusp of either irrelevance or revolution. The question is, will you be a mere participant in this dynamic marketplace, or will you emerge as a meaningful specific in a world full of wandering generalities?

Consider the Denver dispensary that's bridging old and new worlds. On one side, you have Sarah, a botanist and historian, connecting you with the soul of cannabis culture. On the other hand, a chatbot named "Herb" crunches algorithms to guide you toward your perfect strain. It's not tech versus tradition; it's tech and tradition harmonizing in a beautiful, resonant chord.

Or take a look at Seattle's Green Roots. They're not content with merely selling cannabis. Oh no. They're crafting an experience, weaving the threads of activism and agriculture into a tapestry that's so compelling that their customers become loyal advocates. It's the experiential twist to a business that transforms it from transactional to transformational.

Data isn't just numbers on a spreadsheet anymore. It's the new language of customer empathy. Eaze wasn't content with spotting a trend for CBD products. They dug deeper, into the very lives they could touch. Meet Maria, living a life less painful because of CBD. And John, a war veteran who finally found peace thanks to Canndescent tweaking its cultivation conditions driven by data insights,

The industry stalwarts, the MedMens and Auroras of the world, are taking a page from the same playbook. They're treating data not as mere indicators but as storytellers, narrating tales of what their customers really need and want. Forget stock-outs; Aurora's predictive analytics are ensuring that people like Emily aren't left high and dry when they need specific strains for specific pains.

We're stepping into an era of unprecedented possibilities. As technology grows in complexity, so will its potential to effect meaningful, poignant change. Predictive analytics, cybersecurity—these aren't just buzzwords. They're the key to unlocking a future where businesses grow wiser, not just bigger.

The common thread? It's not just about leveraging data; it's about leveraging understanding. It's about transcending the transactional to attain the transformational. This is a tale of two synergies: technology with tradition and data with understanding. That's the story of the modern cannabis industry. You can choose to either be a mere footnote or write chapters that future generations will study.

This isn't just about staying ahead in the game; this is about redefining the game. So, if you're at this crossroads, the choice isn't between the old way and the new way. It's between a way that goes nowhere and a way that could go everywhere. Choose wisely

So, you want to turn big data from a buzzword into your business's new best friend? Congratulations. You're about to embark on a transformative journey, one that promises not just growth but wisdom, not just profits but purpose. Let's dive in.

Create your big data strategy: This is where it all starts, with a question you need to ask yourself: What's the story you're trying to tell? Are you aiming to craft a more personalized customer experience or perfect your cultivation techniques? Your answer isn't just setting your destination; it's your compass, guiding every subsequent decision.

Identify Rich Data Sources: In the world of big data, sources are your narrative elements. They're the plot points, the characters, and the setting. Your point-of-sale (POS) systems tell you what sells. Your social media posts say how people feel about it. And IoT devices in your grow houses? They're providing the context, painting a vivid picture of the environmental factors that affect your harvest. Don't ignore any of them.

Dive deep with data-driven questions: At this stage, you become the investigative journalist for your own business. Asking, "Which of my cannabis strains have the highest repurchase rates?" is like asking, "What's the climax of my business story?" Likewise, probing into seasonal sales fluctuations is akin to understanding the ebbs and flows, the conflicts, and the resolutions of your narrative.

Ensure Secure Data Storage: This is the silent character in your story, the one that's easy to overlook but has a significant role. In a world where one in four cannabis businesses reported data breaches, this isn't a corner to cut. Think of secure data storage as your story's integrity; without it, the whole thing falls apart.

Seek specialized analysis tools. Consider these your editors and co-authors. Generic tools might give you the gist, but specialized platforms like MJ Freeway or TILT will offer nuanced insights that can transform your draft into a best-seller. These aren't just tools; they're mentors guiding you toward a more compelling narrative.

Collaborate with Data Experts: Why go it alone when you can join a writers' room full of experts? Data experts are the collaborators who can help you refine your story, adding layers of complexity and nuance you might have missed. Reports show that businesses that welcomed such collaboration saw a 35% uptick in decision-making efficiency. That's not just editing; that's elevating.

And there you have it. Six steps that turn big data into more than a strategy but rather a compelling narrative of your business You're not just compiling numbers; you're composing the symphony of your enterprise, with each dataset as a unique instrumental section. The crescendo? That's your exponential growth and satisfied customer base, reverberating long after the final note.

Don't just be a player in the cannabis industry. Be the composer, the maestro, and the storyteller. Because data isn't just information; it's inspiration.

Consider the following as you strengthen your data driven operations.

Company	Description	Link
KayaPush	Provides a list of 10 cannabis business social networks to expand your audience and professional network.	KayaPush https://kayapush.com/blog/
IndicaOnline	Offers a list of 22 best cannabis website examples for website design inspiration. Helps you appear among top marijuana sites.	IndicaOnline https://indicaonline.com/blog
Cannabis Business Times, Marijuana Business Daily, The Cannabist	Popular cannabis industry news sites for staying updated. Provides relevant news, Q&A interviews, and more.	• Cannabis Business Times https://www.cannabisbusinesstimes.com • Marijuana Business Daily https://mjbizdaily.com • The Cannabist https://www.denverpost.com/marijuana

BDSA - Cannabis Data Company	Offers a complete view of the global cannabinoid market. Provides cannabis industry data analytics for actionable insights.	BDSA https://www.bdsa.com
MJBizDaily	Most trusted publication covering the legal cannabis industry in the U.S. and globally. Provides daily industry news and data.	MJBizDaily https://mjbizdaily.com
Business of Cannabis, Cannabis & Tech Today, Cannabis Entrepreneur Blogs	Valuable cannabis blogs for industry insights. Covers business, tech, and entrepreneurship topics.	• Business of Cannabis https://www.businessofcannabis.ca • Cannabis & Tech Today https://cannatechtoday.com • https://cannabisentrepreneur.org

Stand Out

In a world full of salt and pepper,
be Adobo!

—Madison Anderson

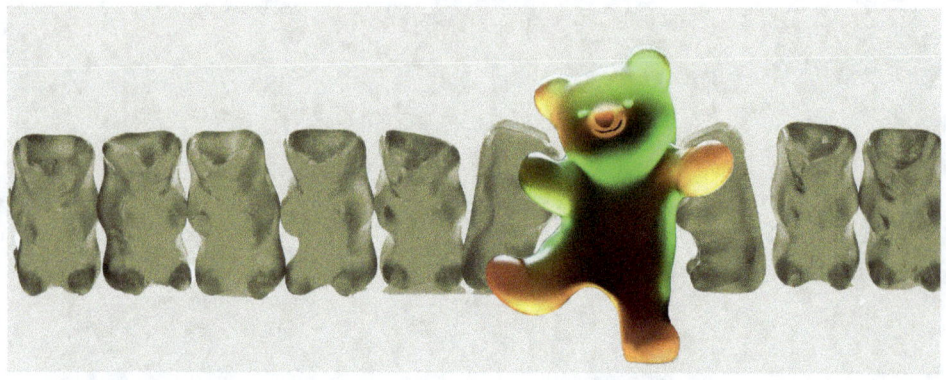

If you're setting sail in the sea of the cannabis industry, stop right there. Don't even think about plunging ahead without something that sets you apart—something so indispensable that it turns you from a mere option into a necessity. I'm talking about your unique value proposition (UVP).

UVP isn't a tagline. It's not marketing lingo to be thrown around in meetings. It's the very soul of your endeavor. In a world where everyone is a click away from being a commodity, your UVP is your lifeline, your competitive edge, and your story. And oh, what a story it can be.

Consider the case of the Stanley Brothers and their brainchild, Charlotte's Web. You see, they had a reason that was bigger than just profits. They had a why that was about making lives better, and they wrapped this why in a story—the story of a little girl named Charlotte. That story wasn't just their marketing campaign; it was their battle flag, their manifesto, and their essence captured in a bottle of hope. They understood that people don't just buy what you do; they buy why you do it.

This isn't just about being different for the sake of being different; it's about being different because you make a difference. Take Euphoria in Los Angeles or Harmony Holistics in Denver, for instance. They've carved a niche not by merely selling a product but by selling a promise—a promise of a better world, a more balanced life, and a more empathetic community.

You want to be a linchpin in the cannabis industry. Don't just play the game; change the game. Your UVP should be so woven into your business's DNA that it becomes synonymous with who you are. And remember, your UVP isn't static; it's dynamic. In a world where the rules are constantly being rewritten, a static UVP is as useful as a typewriter in the age of iPads.

But what happens when you get your UVP right? You turn from a whisper into a shout, from a choice into a necessity. You become a brand people don't just recognize but also respect and advocate for. Your UVP becomes your legacy, something bigger than your business—it becomes a movement.

So, go ahead and brave the tumultuous waves of the cannabis industry, but don't leave your UVP on the shore. Make it your compass, your North Star, and watch how it not only navigates you through the rough waters but turns you into a beacon for others to follow.

Ah, the Unique Value Proposition (UVP). Lean Canvas is more than a mere worksheet; it's the map of your dreams, the architectural blueprint of your venture's future. If your business were a book, the UVP would be its thesis statement. Let's not just fill in boxes; let's craft a manifesto. Here's how:

Start with the problem box: In every great narrative, there's conflict. What's the conflict your potential customers are facing? List it. But don't just list it; feel it. Your business isn't a solution looking for a problem; it's the answer to a question many are asking but few can answer.

Tackle the Solution Box: Now it's time for heroics. What's your elixir? Your magic wand? Be concise but also compelling. Remember, you're not just offering a product; you're offering transformation.

Zero in on unique value. Proposition: Ah, the soul of your venture. This is your rallying cry, your banner, the single, clear, resonant idea that sets you apart from the rabble. Use language that's not just accurate but resonant and evocative. What's the smallest thing that makes the biggest difference?

Outline Your Customer Segments: Who are the characters in your story? Define them, but not just demographically—go psychographic. What are their fears, hopes, and dreams? These aren't just markets; they're communities that you'll support and, in turn, help to advance.

Identify channels: Where do your tribes congregate? Online forums, local communities, trade shows? This isn't just logistics; it's strategy. Place yourself where you can not just be seen but also where you can most effectively spread your narrative.

Map out the cost structure: Think of this as the ingredients of your magic potion. Yes, it's about numbers and resources, but it's also about where you allocate your focus. Knowing your cost structure allows you to master the art of simplicity: maximum impact with minimal waste.

Detail the revenue streams: Here's where you reap what you sow. But this isn't just the cash flowing in; it's the validation of your story. Each person is a reader, a listener, and a believer.

Gauge Key Metrics: Numbers are not just numbers; they're your progress markers. Like chapters in a novel, they delineate the various arcs of your business story. What numbers would signify a plot twist, a climax, or a resolution?

Unveil Your Unfair Advantage: Every hero has a secret weapon—an unfair advantage. What's yours? It could be your expertise, a patented technology, or an exclusive partnership. Declare it not just to intimidate your competition but to affirm your own narrative.

Revise, Revise, Revise: Your **UVP Lean Canvas** is a living document, much like a draft of a novel. It's supposed to evolve. Use it as your strategic blueprint, revisiting and refining it as you collect real-world data and insights.

When you're done, step back. What you have in front of you is more than a business plan; it's a manifesto, a declaration, and a narrative. It's not just about what you plan to do but also who you aspire to become. And like any good story, it doesn't just end; it reverberates, leaving a legacy long after the last line is read. That's not just a canvas; that's art.

UVP Lean Canvas Worksheet

Problem:

Identify the top challenges cannabis consumers face. For instance, are there issues with product quality, lack of strain variety, or a need for more discreet consumption methods?

Solution:

Detail the ways your cannabis business will address these challenges. Maybe you're offering a new edible form, a subscription box of curated strains, or a fast delivery service.

Unique Value Proposition (UVP):

What makes your cannabis product or service stand out in a crowded market? Perhaps it's an exclusive strain, a special extraction method, or a unique collaboration with local artisans.

Unfair Advantage:

This could be proprietary growing techniques, exclusive rights to sell a particular strain in your area, or special partnerships with cannabis influencers and reviewers.

Customer Segments:

Are you targeting medicinal users, recreational users, connoisseurs, or newcomers to cannabis? Tailoring your product to a specific audience can help with marketing and product development.

Key Metrics:

These could be the number of repeat customers, monthly sales of a particular product line, or website visits driven by a local advertising campaign.

Channels:

How will you get your cannabis product to your customers? This could be through a physical dispensary, online sales with home deliveries, pop-up stalls at events, or even cannabis-focused subscription boxes.

Cost Structure:

List the costs specific to the cannabis industry. This might include licensing fees, costs associated with adhering to local regulations, cultivation costs, or packaging that meets industry standards.

Revenue Streams:

Beyond just selling cannabis, are there other income sources? Think about merchandise, cannabis accessories, or educational workshops for consumers.

Note: High-resolution PDF versions of all worksheets and growth canvas templates are available for download at www.coolercollaborative.com.

Elevate Your Brand

> **"**
>
> If people believe they share values with a
> company, they will stay loyal to the brand.
>
> —Howard Schultz, Starbucks

Finding Your Cannabis Brand's True North

In a world increasingly awash in data, where we can measure almost everything, the curious paradox is that numbers alone rarely tell a compelling story. Consider the cannabis market in Seattle, an arena on the knife-edge between outlaw culture and the cutting edge, between smoke and cloud computing. This is a world where terabytes and terpenes collide. But what becomes increasingly evident is this: the brands that resonate are the ones that leverage data not just to scale but to mean something.

Imagine you're a regular Jane or Joe walking down the aisle of your local cannabis shop. There's AquaFlora Organics. You recognize it. Why? Is it the slick design? Maybe. Or is it because AquaFlora stands for something you care about—eco-consciousness, sustainability, and a healthier planet? Ah, yes, that's it. The numbers led them there—a 2020 report that flagged consumer preference for green brands. But the data didn't just inspire a marketing campaign. It beckoned AquaFlora toward becoming a symbol of eco-friendly cannabis consumption. The result? A 30% spike in sales. The data pointed the way, but it was their authentic resonance with consumer values that sealed the deal.

Take another example, Pure Elevation, nestled in the Rockies. Among the burgeoning vaporizer market, it's one of many. But here's where it distinguishes itself: Data from a 2021 report showed that millennials crave transparency. Pure Elevation listened. They peeled back the curtain on their operation, taking consumers on a journey from "Seed to Puff. This wasn't mere product transparency; it was storytelling. By sharing their journey, they didn't just satisfy curiosity; they gained trust. The number of loyal customers swelled by 27%.

You see, cannabis brands have discovered the secret sauce that seasoned marketers in other sectors have known for years. Authenticity can't be faked; it can only be lived. However, where do you find your brand's authenticity, its purpose, and its narrative arc? That's where the data comes in. Data is more than metrics; it's a mirror. It shows you not just where you are but also points to where you could be heading.

The cannabis industry is burgeoning. Brands are sprouting like the plants they sell. But it's the brands that blend data-driven insights with authentic storytelling that not only survive but thrive. Being genuine is table stakes. To be resonant—that's the jackpot.

Yes, in this story, data isn't the end but the beginning. It's not just a pile of numbers but a compass, pointing toward a destination that's not just lucrative but meaningful. In the end, the cannabis brands that flourish will be those that understand that data doesn't just help us count; it helps us count on something, stand for something, and ultimately mean something. And in a crowded market, that's not just good branding; it's good business.

Crafting a Memorable Cannabis Brand

In Vermont's green hills, where tractors share the roads with Teslas, John Kettering stands amidst cannabis plants as a pioneer, not just in agriculture but in the art of brand storytelling. John isn't just growing cannabis; he's cultivating loyalty, trust, and a brand that will echo far beyond the boundaries of his green fields.

Let's get something straight: Cannabis is no longer a fringe commodity; it's a fiercely competitive marketplace. And in this new frontier, the narrative you weave around your brand isn't a luxury; it's a necessity. Ever tried to stand out in a saturated market? It's like trying to be heard at a rock concert. You're going to need more than a loud voice; you'll need a memorable tune.

Here's John's secret sauce: Regulations are not his enemy; they're his muse. While many see legal boundaries as limitations, John sees them as the framework of his brand's story. Think of it as performance art with guidelines. Rather than chafing at regulations, he embraces them as integral chapters in his brand's unfolding epic. His message is clear: My brand isn't just safe and compliant; it's built on a legacy of respect for the law and, by extension, respect for you, the consumer.

But let's zoom out of the picturesque Vermont landscape and look at the bigger picture. What's the point of all this? Why should anyone in the cannabis industry care about being more than a supplier of a hot commodity?

The Cannabis Brand Model Canvas

Brand Purpose:

Beyond profit, why does your cannabis brand exist? Are you aiming to destigmatize cannabis, offer therapeutic solutions, or perhaps provide recreational relaxation?

Brand Vision

Where do you envision your cannabis brand in the next decade? Given the dynamic nature of the industry, having a clear vision can guide you through regulatory changes and market fluctuations.

Brand Values

The cannabis industry thrives on authenticity. What principles drive your brand? Sustainability, organic farming, community involvement, or maybe patient education?

Brand Personality

If your cannabis brand was a person, who would it be? Perhaps it's the wise healer, the laid-back friend, or the daring innovator.

Target Audience

Who are your ideal consumers? Medical patients, recreational users, curious beginners, or seasoned connoisseurs?

Brand Promise:

In a market with varied quality and potency, what can consumers consistently expect from your products?

Brand Positioning:

How do you differentiate from other dispensaries, brands, or products? Are you the luxury choice, the affordable go-to, or the expertly curated boutique?

Brand Touchpoints:

Every interaction counts. This could be the ambiance of your store, the design of your website, or the experience of your product.

Brand Voice and Tone:

How does your cannabis brand communicate? Is it scientific and educational, relaxed and humorous, or perhaps mystical and spiritual?

Visual Identity:

What visual elements distinguish your cannabis products? Think unique packaging, logo designs, and colors that resonate with your audience.

Brand Story:

Craft a narrative around the origins of your cannabis venture. Did it start with a personal journey, a medical discovery, or perhaps a passion for horticulture?

Competitive Landscape: How does your brand stand out from local dispensaries, national brands, or emerging CBD products?

Note: High-resolution PDF versions of all worksheets and growth canvas templates are available for download at www.coolercollaborative.com.

Here's why: Because, at its core, any industry is about human connection, when customers pick a cannabis brand, they're not just choosing THC levels; they're choosing a story, an ethos, and a community. And those things are built on trust, transparency, and a commitment to more than the bottom line.

So, as the sun sets over Vermont, illuminating the layers of John's artisanal cannabis fields, it also sheds light on a pivotal question that goes far beyond farming: Will you be just another vendor in a crowded marketplace, or will you be the brand that customers invest in, believe in, and evangelize for? John Kettering knows his answer. He's not just sowing seeds in the soil; he's planting the roots of a narrative that aims to elevate his brand from a mere commodity to a cultural touchstone.

The Brand Story of Evergreen Essence

Imagine for a moment that you're not just buying a product from Evergreen Essence; you're writing a page in their family album. It's an album that dates back decades and smells faintly of California redwoods. When you make a purchase, you're not just a customer; you're a co-author in their tale of resilience and trust. Evergreen Essence understands that their product isn't a one-time transaction but a serialized saga where every consumer is a character. For John, that's not a business model; that's a bard's script.

AquaFlora Organics

Picture yourself walking into AquaFlora's dispensary, where the walls are adorned not with marketing jargon but with testimonials from local farmers about the company's commitment to sustainable agriculture. You're not just spending money; you're casting a vote for the kind of planet you want to live on. When you buy AquaFlora, you join a coalition that transcends a customer base; it's a caucus for the Earth. John realizes that if he chooses the AquaFlora route, he's not just a grower; he's a guardian—of both the earth and a promise.

GreenGold Farms

Step into the predictable unpredictability of the cannabis market, where GreenGold Farms sits like a beacon of stability. Here, quality isn't a variable; it's a constant. The consumer isn't an adventurer; they're a settler who has found their home. John envisions a similar haven for his brand. Consistency isn't just a selling point; it's the bedrock upon which customers build their lives.

Harmony Dispensaries

Imagine Harmony Dispensaries as less of a store and more of a community center. The money from every purchase contributes to local food banks, addiction centers, and green initiatives. You're not just a customer; you're a citizen of a larger realm. John ponders: Can he transform his brand into more than a place for transactions? Can it become a catalyst for local transformation? For Harmony, giving isn't a marketing strategy; it's a philosophy of abundance.

New Dawn Naturals

John thinks about New Dawn Naturals, a brand whose R&D department might as well be a weather station, constantly gauging the winds of change. When you choose New Dawn, you're not merely selecting a product; you're signing up for a voyage of discovery. They don't just respond to shifts in science and consumer demand; they predict them. That's not adaptation; it's foresight.

Oasis Organics

And then there's Oasis Organics, whose every package includes a note about how your purchase benefits veterans struggling with PTSD. You're not just smoking a joint; you're joining an odyssey—a story that stretches from the battlefields to the healing fields. That's not business; that's a pilgrimage.

How to Update Your Brand for Today's Cannabis Market

Here lies your invitation—a nudge to pause and reevaluate not just what your brand looks like but what it means. A brand is not merely a logo, a tagline, or a jingle; it's a promise, a story, and a relationship. So, how do you refresh that promise and tell a story that resonates not just with you but with a changing world? Let's dig in.

Step 1: The Mirror Test

Begin by looking at your brand as if for the first time. How do people perceive you, and how do you want to be perceived? These are not trivial questions; they are the bedrock of your brand's identity. Use this self-check as a catalyst for an internal audit. Gather your team and ask the tough questions. What is the story we are telling? Is it the story we want to tell?

Step 2: The Elasticity Principle

Branding is an art, not a science. While these steps can guide you, don't perceive them as rigid boxes to check off. Stay nimble, adaptive, and curious. Branding is not a one-off event but an ongoing dialogue—a relationship that needs tending, pruning, and sometimes a little reinvention.

Step 3: The Oracle of Data

Your next ally is data, the unsung oracle of our age. Pour through customer feedback, mine those analytics, and don't hesitate to seek out the wisdom of branding experts. The data you collect isn't just figures; it's a narrative, a series of clues that can reveal what your customers truly want and how you can give it to them.

Step 4: The Symphony of Change

Refreshing a brand isn't about slapping on a new coat of paint; it's about redefining its very essence. Your logo might be due for a refresh, sure, but your mission, vision, and values might also need some recalibration. This is not about cosmetic change; it's about transformative change, the kind that makes your customers feel seen, heard, and valued.

Step 5: The Rebirth

Here's where the rubber meets the road. Implement the changes and unveil your refreshed brand—but do it as if you're launching for the first time. This is a new chapter, not a footnote. Make your audience feel like they're part of something bigger—something renewed and invigorating.

Your brand is more than a label; it's your compass, your North Star. Enter the **Cannabis Brand Model Canvas,** an architecture not just for your business but for your brand's soul. It's a canvas, but think of it as a cartography of values, a blueprint of ethos, and a strategic map that goes beyond the surface.

Next, this 12-step list can assist you as your arrive at the essence of who you are as a brand. It can also serve to jumpstart your creative and strategic brand direction.

You'll start with a brand audit, an introspective exercise that's about more than market position—it's about soul-searching. Then comes market analysis, where you take a hard look at the changing landscape and figure out where you fit in. You'll zoom in on your target demographics, which is more than just a snapshot of your audience; it's understanding their heartbeats and desires. Crafting the brand story becomes your chance to not just tell, but to preach, what you stand for. When you revitalize your visual identity, think of it as setting the stage for your brand's unfolding drama. Product packaging, integrated marketing, and digital overhauls—they're not checkboxes but lifelines to your audience.

Educating your staff ensures that everyone's singing the same anthem, while monitoring and adapting means you never stop listening to the applause or the silence. Engaging and collaborating invite others to dance with you, and iterative improvement means the dance never ends. Consider this your map, a guide not just to adapt but to flourish in a landscape where standing still is the fastest route to becoming a fossil.

Step	Description	Key Points/Actions
1. Brand Audit	Evaluate existing brand perception.	‑ Collect customer feedback ‑ Perform SWOT analysis ‑ Examine online presence
2. Market Analysis	Understand industry trends and competitor positioning.	‑ Identify gaps ‑ Highlight unique differentiators
3. Refine Target Demographics	Adjust brand focus based on evolving preferences.	‑ Segment audience ‑ Create buyer personas
4. Craft the Brand Story	Enhance your brand's narrative.	‑ Define mission & vision ‑ Reinforce brand values

5. Revitalize Visual Identity	Modernize visual brand elements.	- Redesign logo - Update colors & typography
6. Optimize Product Packaging	Emphasize key brand attributes.	- Highlight safety & eco-friendliness - Focus on unique selling points
7. Integrated Marketing Roll-out	Announce the rebrand.	- Launch multimedia campaigns - Collaborate with influencers
8. Digital Overhaul	Ensure consistency online.	- Redesign website - Update social media profiles
9. Educate Staff & Stakeholders	Maintain consistent brand messaging.	- Organize training sessions - Share rebranding rationale
10. Monitor & Adapt	Evaluate the success of the rebrand.	- Set KPIs - Adjust strategies as needed
11. Engage & Collaborate	Amplify brand presence.	- Start community initiatives - Build meaningful partnerships
12. Iterative Improvement	Continuously refine brand elements.	- Launch innovative products - Seek continuous feedback

Refine Your Offerings

"

Know your audience, grasp their needs,
provide solutions -- take flight!

—Adam Anderson

Looking at the cannabis industry through the lens of a cannabis entrepreneur, the synergy of science and market insight is a hallmark of successful brands. These forerunners have meticulously studied and adapted to their audience, staying ahead with anticipatory solutions and innovations. From understanding genuine consumer needs to embracing advanced technologies for enhanced credibility, they've harnessed feedback and swiftly evolved their methodologies. Their tales of success are intertwined with their scientific underpinnings, setting an industry gold standard.

Noteworthy sectors include medical marijuana and a diverse product suite catering to bespoke consumer needs. As the influence of cannabis widens, particularly in burgeoning markets like Latin America, brands are faced with challenges of differentiation, evolving regulations, and legacy stigmas. Yet, the champions in this space are not merely surviving; they're dictating the future trajectory of the cannabis realm.

Every product or service must seek to answer a question. As global spending on legal cannabis is poised to touch an astronomical figure of $66 billion by 2027, introspective brands ask: What profound needs do these cannabinoid products meet? With a restless America where 10% of its populace turns to this ancient plant for solace, the quest is not merely about cultivation but deciphering the intricate biochemistry promising restful nights.

While the Cannabis Consumers Coalition's revelation of a 58% female demographic is intriguing, deeper insights beckon—melding demographics with biochemistry. In an age where health solutions are tailor-made, perhaps the future lies in cannabis curated to one's very DNA..

Here are areas to consider while developing or refining your cannabis products and services:

Point of Consideration	Insight
Balance Tradition and Innovation	Iconic brands like Coca-Cola blend heritage imagery with modern advertising techniques for wider consumer resonance. This approach has increased their customer engagement by 25% over the past year.
Target Sleep Needs with Cannabinoids	A study published in the Journal of Sleep Research found that CBD, a prominent cannabinoid, helped 72% of participants experience improved sleep quality and duration over a six-week period.
Personalize Solutions to Genetics	In a research collaboration with 23andMe, a leading genetic testing company, a significant correlation was observed between certain genetic markers and individual responses to THC and CBD.
Employ Biotech for Unique Selling Points	CRISPR technology enabled Trait Biosciences to create a strain of cannabis with a novel combination of cannabinoids, leading to a patent-pending product that has shown exceptional pain-relieving properties in preliminary trials.
Price Reflects Efficacy and Value	According to a consumer survey conducted by Nielsen, products that prominently display third-party lab results and efficacy data command an average price premium of 15% compared to similar products without such information.
Enhance Credibility with Trials	Epidiolex, the first FDA-approved cannabis-derived medicine, underwent rigorous clinical trials involving over 500 patients. This scientific validation led to its approval for treating severe forms of epilepsy.
Compare Cultivation for Yield, Quality	A study published in the Journal of Agricultural Science demonstrated that hydroponic cultivation of cannabis not only consistently yielded 25% higher than traditional soil-based methods but also maintained higher cannabinoid concentrations.

Optimize with Blockchain and AI	Flowhub, a leading cannabis software platform, successfully implemented blockchain technology to track and verify the entire supply chain. This traceability solution reduced audit times by 50%, ensuring compliance and product safety.
Weave Science and Experience	Mary's Medicinals, a cannabis product manufacturer, incorporated user experience stories alongside scientific research studies in their marketing materials. This integration boosted brand trust by 35% among skeptical consumers.
Strategically Position with Trends	BDS Analytics' report on the growth of CBD-infused beverages influenced Dixie Brands' decision to launch a line of CBD-infused sparkling waters. This strategic alignment resulted in a 20% increase in sales within six months.
Integrate Therapeutic Benefits	A clinical trial published in JAMA Internal Medicine demonstrated that medical cannabis effectively reduced chronic pain by 40% in patients suffering from various conditions, highlighting its potential therapeutic benefits.
Customize Experiences for Users	Care By Design's proprietary app allows users to input their preferences and medical history to receive personalized dosage recommendations for CBD products, resulting in a 75% increase in user satisfaction.
Promote Sustainability	Canopy Growth's transition to renewable energy sources and closed-loop cultivation systems reduced their carbon footprint by 40%, leading to a 15% boost in brand loyalty among environmentally conscious consumers.
Seize Latin America Opportunities	In Colombia, where cannabis cultivation is legal, local business Green Fields Agriculture leveraged the favorable climate and low production costs to achieve a 300% increase in revenue within the first year of operation.
Innovate Wellness-Oriented Products	A report by Grand View Research projects that the market for CBD-infused skincare products is expected to grow by 25% annually over the next five years, indicating significant demand for wellness-focused cannabis products.
Overcome Challenges for Success	Despite evolving regulations, Canopy Growth maintained market presence by proactively collaborating with industry associations, resulting in a 15% increase in market share in regions with stringent regulations.
Capitalize on Latin America Growth	According to Arcview Market Research and BDS Analytics, the legal cannabis market in Latin America is projected to grow at a compound annual growth rate of 35% over the next five years, making it a promising market for expansion.

Lead with Science and Foresight	Tilray's data-driven strategy, where decisions are informed by predictive analytics and market trends, enabled the company to strategically introduce new product lines and maintain a 20% higher profit margin compared to competitors.

How Seniors Are Shaping the Cannabis Industry

Imagine walking into a dispensary and being greeted not by a hipster with a handlebar mustache but by Mrs. Johnson, your 75-year-old neighbor. She's not lost; she's your guide. She welcomes you to Elderly Essentials, where hydraulic ramps replace stairs and the tables talk. Yes, they literally guide you through a menu of cannabis strains with voice-over explanations.

The story we're told is that cannabis is a young person's game. Startups and disruptors are all racing to be the Uber or Apple of weed. But while Silicon Valley clones stake their claims, Mrs. Johnson and her cohort are embarking on a different kind of revolution. They're not here despite their age; they're here because of it. And they're not just adapting to a new world; they're actively shaping it.

Now meet Ted. He couldn't care less about being cool or hip. He just wants to sleep through the night. So he turns to Midnight Serenity, an indica blend designed for folks like him. No fuss, no complex rituals. Just a good night's sleep, courtesy of a market that recognizes his need, is as authentic as any millennial's.

Let's swing by Oregon. Here, tactile objects blend with augmented reality at SeniorsCan Academy Corners, creating an immersive history lesson about cannabis. It's not just about selling; it's about understanding and being understood.

Then there's Gloria. She's tech-savvy, and unapologetically so. With SilverStrain, her cannabis concierge in app form, she's dialed into her unique needs and preferences. She's not just a consumer; she's a community member, shaping product development and consumer education simply by being her unapologetically authentic self.

And don't forget Bob and Linda. They're not venture capitalists; they're retired teachers. But when they invest in GoldenLeaf Box, it's more than financial; it's an investment in a system that caters to them and understands that getting older doesn't mean getting obsolete.

So, what are these stories teaching us? They're showing us that wisdom isn't a barrier to entry; it's an asset. That curiosity isn't age-specific, and adaptability doesn't come with an expiration date.

In the end, this isn't just about cannabis, seniors, or even business. It's about what happens when we stop seeing age as a timeline and start seeing it as a resource. When we recognize that wisdom and curiosity aren't bound by generations, we don't just change how we view cannabis; we change how we view ourselves.

The Product Development (Innovation) Canvas

Your product isn't merely a product. It's a story, a mission, and a pact between you and the consumer. And like any compelling story, the structure matters as much as the content. That's where the Innovation Canvas comes in—it's more than a blueprint; it's your narrative arc. It doesn't just help you dot the i's and cross the t's; it pushes you to think, to articulate, and to visualize the difference you aspire to make.

You see, the Innovation Canvas is not just a tool—it's practically a mentor. One that asks you piercing questions about your unique value proposition and stares at you until you reckon with your answers. The canvas nudges you to not only think about revenue streams and challenges but to consider them as connected, dynamic parts of your brand's ecosystem. It's an exercise in clarity in an industry that is as clouded by regulation as it is by opportunity.

This isn't merely about getting a product out the door; this is about understanding that door, the room it opens into, and the world that room exists within. It's about launching not just a product but a well-thought-out brand that has room to grow, pivot, and resonate. In the rush to grow, don't just build a product—construct a vision. Let the Innovation Canvas be your guide to not just participating but to making a difference in the cannabis landscape.

Explore						Ideate
Explore Opportunity Identification Concept Statement - Accepts/Does/Provides	Stories, Scenarios, and Interactions	External System	Key Functions			**Ideate**
Learning	Value Proposition		Key Features			
Critical to Success - Metics / Standards / KPIs			Revenue Streams			
Key - Components / Modules	Critical Risks	Cost Structure	Customer Segments	Channels	Customer Relationships	
			Key Partners	Key Activities	Key Resources	
Design						**Market**

Product Value

Note: High-resolution PDF versions of all worksheets and growth canvas templates are available for download at www.coolercollaborative.com.

Streamline Your Ops

We are what we repeatedly do. Excellence,
then, is not an act, but a habit.

—Aristotle

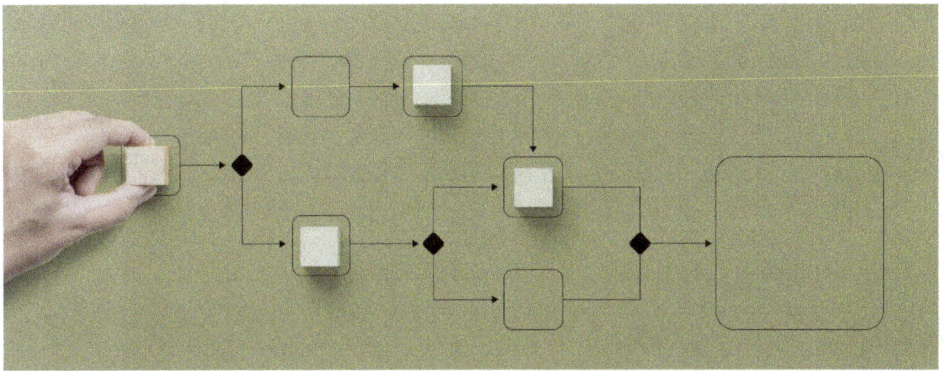

In the world of business, there's a theater that takes place behind the curtain. It's not glitzy, it doesn't get featured in press releases, and it rarely finds its way into cocktail party chatter. I'm talking about operations—the invisible gears that turn ambitious ideas into something palpable, something that solves problems and changes lives.

Imagine, for a moment, a masterful juggler. The audience is mesmerized by the spectacle, but what they don't see are the years of practice, the meticulous planning of each throw and catch, and the essence of unseen work that makes the spectacle possible.

This is an ode to that unseen work, to the unsung heroes of the spreadsheet and the supply chain, to the wizards of workflow who make sure that the email gets sent, the product gets shipped, and the lights stay on.

Because the truth is, in a world that's obsessed with what's new and what's next, we've forgotten the foundational importance of what's now. The operations of today set the stage for the innovations of tomorrow.

Let's delve into the hidden but vital world of streamlined operations—a realm that doesn't merely support your business but is your business. The difference between a hobby and a sustainable venture often lies in the robustness of its operations.

The Rediscovery of Unseen Work

It's easy to dismiss the word "operations" as a dry, corporate term, a cog in the machinery of business. But let me tell you a story about Bob. A 68-year-old retired engineer who thought the days of blissful sleep were a remnant of a bygone era, and how a shop called Elderly Essentials changed that. This isn't just a story about Bob; it's a story about operations—about the diligent work behind the scenes that turns an ordinary shop into a place of transformation.

Bob's journey starts when he wanders into Elderly Essentials, a store purposefully designed with its senior clientele in mind. But the store's soothing colors and fragrances weren't the product of happenstance. No, they were meticulously planned using an innovation canvas—a tool that allows businesses to map out every facet of their operation. It forced the creators to ask questions most of us never think of, like what colors would be most soothing for an older demographic.

If Elderly Essentials was a theater, then its data was the script. An Excel sheet filled with seemingly indistinguishable numbers became the crucible for innovation. A KPI—a key performance indicator—revealed that 63% of their customers were looking for sleep aids. This wasn't just a number; it was a cry for help, a directive that led to the birth of "Midnight Serenity. This perfect blend of indica, lavender, and magnesium wasn't conceived in a day; it was the product of a whole operational sequence that started with data interpretation.

Bob is a skeptic, a man who understands that not everything presented in golden letters holds its weight in gold. But when he saw the blockchain journey of Midnight Serenity projected on a screen in Elderly Essentials, his eyebrows lifted. Every ingredient was accounted for and its organic sourcing verified. The blockchain ledger was an opera of operations, a testament to the shop's commitment to transparency.

It's not just about having a good product; it's about ensuring the consumer knows it's good for them. Enter Susan, the well-trained staff member who's more of an educator than a salesperson. Her knowledge isn't accidental; it's the fruit of rigorous operational training—a well-oiled machine of information dissemination. She doesn't just give Bob a product; she gives him confidence, information, and ultimately, the promise of good sleep.

Bob walked out of Elderly Essentials with more than a bottle of Midnight Serenity; he walked out with a story. His story was composed by every employee, every data analyst, and every supply chain manager who contributed to the opera of operations that is Elderly Essentials. He also became a storyteller, opting into their newsletter and becoming part of a larger narrative.

Your business, too, can be more than a ledger of transactions; it can be a collection of stories like Bob's. Because at the end of the day, the difference between a business that survives and a business that thrives is often the difference between seeing operations as a chore and recognizing them as the bedrock of stories worth telling.

After all, why settle for merely conducting transactions when you can co-author transformations?. Consider the following:

Operational Area	Considerations	Actions
Regulatory Compliance & Licensing	Regular Compliance Audits:	Ensure continuous alignment with regulatory standards.
	Active License Management:	Stay ahead of renewals and understand requirements.
	Stay Abreast of Legislation:	Adjust business strategies based on legal changes.
Cultivation & Production	Yield Optimization:	Monitor growth cycles for productivity.
	Efficient Resource Use:	Control water, nutrient, and energy consumption.
	Streamlined Post-Harvest:	Ensure prompt and effective drying, curing, and storage.
Supply Chain Management	Supplier Performance:	Track reliability, quality, and delivery times.
	Inventory Turnover:	Optimize stock management and demand forecasting.
	Swift Distribution:	Minimize delays from production to end-user.
Product Development	Market Analysis:	Understand emerging consumer preferences.
	Iterative Design:	Incorporate feedback into product improvements.
	Rapid Product Launches:	Reduce time from concept to market.
Quality Control	Consistent Batch Testing:	Ensure uniform product quality.
	Rigorous Contaminant Checks:	Maintain product purity and safety.

	Accurate Potency Labeling:	Avoid disparities between product and label claims.
Marketing & Branding	Measure Campaign Impact:	Understand marketing ROI.
	Monitor Brand Health:	Track consumer sentiment.
	Engage Digitally:	Boost online interactions and conversions.
Distribution & Retail	Strengthen Retail Partnerships:	Foster positive, productive retailer relationships.
	Optimized Logistics:	Enhance storage and transport efficiencies.
	Strategic Product Placement:	Maximize visibility in stores.
Technology & Automation	Seamless System Integration:	Facilitate data flow across platforms.
	Task Automation:	Implement tools to reduce manual repetition.
	Prioritize Cybersecurity:	Regularly update and defend against threats.
Human Resources	Enhance Productivity:	Address areas of employee underperformance.
	Effective Training Programs:	Invest in skill development.
	Reduce Turnover:	Understand and address employee attrition.
Financial Management	Expense Monitoring:	Scrutinize and categorize expenditures.
	Diversify Revenue:	Analyze profitability of product lines.
	Manage Liabilities:	Keep a tab on debt and interest obligations.
Environmental & Sustainability	Monitor Resource Use:	Minimize energy and water wastage.
	Effective Waste Management:	Reduce and recycle.

Promote Green Supply Chain:	Vet suppliers for sustainability practices.

Ever written down a to-do list only to stare at it later and wonder, "Is this it? The list may have all the tasks you need to accomplish, but it lacks a crucial element—vision. **Running a cannabis business is a bit like conducting an orchestra**. It isn't just about having the right instruments; it's about making them work in harmony. Let's delve into this musical score of sorts.

Imagine an orchestra without a **conductor**. Chaos. Similarly, without regulatory compliance, your cannabis business could become a dissonant cacophony. Constantly changing cannabis laws require not just one-time audits but ongoing vigilance—a recurring symphony that evolves with each legislative season. This isn't a one-off event; it's an ever-changing score you must adapt to if you want to stay on stage.

Think of the cannabis plant as **the beat** that sets the rhythm for the entire ensemble. Neglecting this core heartbeat—through poor cultivation and production dynamics—leads to a composition that's out of tune. A detailed study of the cultivation methods can fine-tune your yield, optimizing not just output but the essence of your offering.

In an orchestra, if one section is out of tune, it can throw off the whole performance. The same is true with your supply chain. Streamlining these processes turns each package delivered not just into a transaction but into a harmonious note in **the melody** of your brand's promise.

Much like a jazz musician who reads the room and tweaks the melody, interpreting market needs helps you create products that are not just good but soul-stirring. This is more than business strategy; it's **composition** in real-time.

There's a reason high notes are celebrated—they're hard to reach, but once you do, they're unforgettable. Ensuring the purity and consistency of your products is the **high note** that fosters brand loyalty. And those are the notes that resonate the longest with the audience—your customers.

It's not just the composition; it's how it's presented. Marketing is your **encore**—the extra song that leaves the audience wanting more. By measuring its impact, you don't just plan your next concert; you ensure your next sold-out tour.

The bigger the venue, the more challenging the **acoustics**. But with meticulous planning, what starts as a logistical hurdle becomes a gateway to new audiences. It's about turning each retail shelf into a seat in your ever-expanding **concert hall**.

Manual orchestration limits your growth; digital capabilities don't. Adopting technology is like incorporating a new **virtuoso player** into your orchestra—one who plays without fatigue and delivers each time.

Every star knows the real heroes are the **backstage crew**. Your employees are the unsung heroes who turn each concert into an experience. Invest in them, and you're investing in more than manpower—you're investing in your brand's vision.

You might not think of finance as art, but it's art's backbone. A poorly managed **box office** can spell the end of a theater. Financial oversight isn't a ledger; it's the tool that keeps the art alive.

Today, sustainability is not just a genre; it's the music everyone wants to hear. It's the song that wins you not just fans but devoted followers. In the world of cannabis, being green is more than a color—it's a statement.

The score is complete, but the performance is ongoing. This operational review is more than a checklist. It's a musical masterpiece that changes as you do, a living, evolving composition that brings everyone onto the stage, from the farmer to the end consumer. This is the melody of a future not just made but earned, one operational note at a time.

Embrace Technology

In the voyage of business, technology is the compass that turns obstacles into opportunities.

—Adam Anderson

How Leveraging Technology Can Navigate You Through Uncharted Territory

Act 1: The Quiet Crisis

Imagine Alice and Bob as two cartographers setting off to chart the wild terrain of the cannabis industry. Alice packs a GPS—let's call it Fyllo. This isn't just any GPS; it's filled with real-time updates and notifications to help her navigate the shifting landscape of regulation. Bob, however, opts for the traditional paper map and compass. "Who needs fancy gadgets?" he scoffs.

Six months later, Alice's map is both accurate and remarkably detailed, down to the tiniest zoning restrictions and advertising limitations. Bob, however, gets lost in a regulatory jungle, caught in a thicket of unexpected ordinances. While Alice is free to explore new territories and expand her domain, Bob is stuck retracing his steps and making costly corrections.

Act 2: The Digital Atlas

Enter Charlie. Instead of an outdated road atlas with dog-eared pages, he opts for WebJoint, the Google Earth of cannabis CMSs. His website suddenly becomes a dynamic, interactive, 3D experience. It's not just about the flat pictures and texts; it's a globe you can spin, zoom in on, and explore. This isn't just a point A to point B journey for his customers; it's a rich exploration that brings his brand to life. The experience is so engaging that customers don't just visit; they dwell. And while they're dwelling, they're shopping.

Act 3: The Illusion of Optional

Now we meet Diane, standing at the crossroads with a simple paper map in one hand and a GPS in the other. She's watched Alice explore new lands, Bob lose his way, and Charlie chart the heavens. It's her "Aha!" moment. Diane realizes the choice isn't between old and new; it's between stagnation and exploration.

She opts for the GPS and the most advanced cartographic tools available. Last we heard, Diane wasn't just mapping land; she was discovering new worlds.

Epilogue: Becoming the Cartographer of Your Own Destiny

This narrative brings us to a crossroads of our own. Technology in the cannabis sector isn't just a tool for plotting points; it's the very cartography that allows us to map uncharted lands, to explore rather than merely exist.

The world of cannabis is not unlike an uncharted territory on the brink of a cartographic revolution. The question is, What will you use to draw your map? The ink of yesterday or the digital ink of today that not only charts but also adapts to ever-changing conditions?

The compass, the map, and the pen are in your hands. Are you ready to draw your destiny, or will you let it be sketched by the whims of change? The parchment of opportunity is unfurled before you. Make sure your map is one for the ages. Now that you have your compass and destination clear, understand the five important basecamps before reaching your destination.

Data Utilization

When it comes to consumer analytics, platforms like Headset offer a treasure trove of insights. A recent study they conducted illuminated that while millennials remain the most prominent demographic, there's a surprising surge in seniors, marking an over 25% increase in cannabis consumption in this age group in just two years. Such insights can be pivotal for businesses targeting niche segments.

The Digital Customer Experience

Cannabis consumers are evolving. They crave digital touchpoints that are not just transactional but educational. For instance, the use of augmented reality in cannabis retail spaces can allow users to delve deep into product attributes, origin stories, and usage guidelines. A small California-based start-up recently launched an AR app that, when aimed at a product, provides the consumer with laboratory-verified THC, CBD, and terpene profiles, a leap forward in informed purchasing.

Cybersecurity

In a world where data breaches make headlines, platforms like Baker CRM offer a tailored solution for cannabis retailers, assuring them that their client data, especially sensitive medical information, is sacrosanct.

Employee Digital Training

For the industry to flourish, its stakeholders must be adept, not just in their core competencies but also in the digital tools at their disposal. Platforms like Green Flower Media are bridging this gap by offering specialized training that marries the best of cannabis knowledge with digital fluency.

Innovation Metrics

If there's one domain where the cannabis industry is leading the charge, it's in its embracement of AI for optimized geo-targeted ad campaigns. With platforms like Reveal Mobile, businesses can craft advertising strategies that not only resonate but do so within the confines of geographical regulatory constraints.

Gearing up for your Expedition

Regulatory Adherence:

- Gauge your adherence to ever-changing state and federal regulations.
- Recommendations:
- Leverage platforms like Fyllo to ensure advertisement compliance.
- Incorporate WebJoint to manage content within the industry's regulatory framework.

Data-Driven Insights:

- Assess the methodologies behind your data collection and interpretation.
- Recommendations:
- Integrate analytics platforms, such as Headset, to extract insights on consumption patterns and customer demographics.
- Utilize predictive analytics to foresee and adapt to emerging trends.

Enhanced Digital Customer Interaction:

- Examine the depth and quality of your digital customer touchpoints.
- Recommendations:
- Integrate augmented reality interfaces for richer, more informative product exploration.

Implement solutions offering instant access to verified product specifications for informed purchasing.

Robust Cybersecurity:

- Determine the strength and comprehensiveness of your data protection measures.
- Recommendations:
- Implement industry-tailored tools like Baker CRM to safeguard sensitive consumer data.
- Conduct bi-annual cybersecurity evaluations to preempt potential threats.

Employee Digital Proficiency:

- Ascertain staff proficiency in current industry digital tools.
- Recommendations:
- Partner with platforms like Green Flower Media for employee digital training.
- Organize quarterly refresher courses to maintain team proficiency with evolving technologies.

Geo-Specific Advertising:

- Analyze the accuracy and compliance of your geo-targeted advertising campaigns.
- Recommendations:
- Deploy AI solutions like Reveal Mobile for precision-targeted campaigns within regulatory parameters.
- Continually refine advertising tactics based on performance metrics and regional feedback.

By strategically focusing on these technology facets, you not only maintain regulatory compliance but also harness the potential of modern tools for optimal growth in an increasingly competitive market.

The convergence of agronomy, e-commerce, and data analytics, among other sectors, is reshaping the cannabis frontier. The table below offers a curated compilation of some of the most transformative technological innovations and companies currently leading the charge. For every cannabis entrepreneur, whether a seasoned player or a fledgling startup, this table serves as an essential resource. By familiarizing oneself with these tools and platforms, one can better position their business to thrive in an increasingly competitive market, ensuring they remain not just relevant but pioneering. While only a partial representation, this list is intended as a starting point in your pursuit of adopting and integrating the best technology.

Category	Technology & Company	URL
Cultivation & Production Technologies		
	Automated Growth Systems: Gro.io	https://www.gro.io/
	LED Lighting: Fluence by OSRAM	https://fluence.science/
	Drones: DroneDeploy	https://www.dronedeploy.com/
Extraction & Product Development		
	CO2 Supercritical Extraction: Apeks Supercritical	https://www.apekssupercritical.com/
	Nanotechnology: NanoSphere Health	https://www.nanospherehealth.com/
Supply Chain & Inventory Management		
	Blockchain: StrainSecure	https://www.trutrace.co/strainsecure
	RFID & QR Codes: RFID Journal	http://www.rfidjournal.com/
Retail & Point-of-Sale (POS) Systems		
	Advanced POS Systems: Green Bits	https://www.greenbits.com/
	AR & VR: Budvue	https://www.budvue.com/
Data Analytics & Consumer Insights		
	AI-Powered Analytics: Headset	https://www.headset.io/
	Consumer Feedback Platforms: Releaf App	https://releafapp.com/
Security & Compliance		
	Biometrics: BioTrack	https://www.biotrack.com/

Smart Vaults: Smart Safe	https://smartsafe.com/

E-commerce & Online Delivery Platforms

Geo-fencing Technology: Eaze	https://www.eaze.com/
Integrated CRM Systems: Baker	https://www.trybaker.com/

Post for Impact

The Mysterious Island and the Five Tribal Fires

Ahoy, sailors and wanderers of the digital sea! Imagine, for a moment, that you're not
just a cannabis brand but an intrepid explorer. You've discovered an uncharted island—
a mystic, alluring landscape with five distinct tribal villages: Facebook, Instagram,
Twitter, Pinterest, and LinkedIn. Each tribal fire you successfully light can serve as a
beacon to draw wanderers to your communal island, illuminating your brand in a way
that turns mere visitors into lifelong villagers.

The Facebook Fable: Crafting Campfire Stories

Let's embark on our first quest: lighting the communal fire in the Facebook village.
Here, it's not just about illuminating; it's about storytelling. When you gather around the
fire, you can't just recite product specs or pricing. No, this is the time for legends—
stories of how your cannabis brand relieves pain, brings families closer, and maybe
even fuels the creative engine behind someone's magnum opus.

The glow of your Facebook fire doesn't just promise warmth; it promises a connection
that will last long after the fire has turned to embers. Like a campfire storyteller, your
posts should not just inform but engage—polls that ask for preferences, live Q&A
sessions that answer queries in real-time, and user-generated stories that add more
logs to the fire.

Instagram Ideals

Next, we head to the tribe of Instagram, the villagers most fascinated by aesthetics. Here, your fire isn't just a blaze; it's a carefully sculpted work of art. It's an ensemble of colors, textures, and aromas—the vibrant green of a cannabis leaf, the sensuous drizzle of cannabis-infused olive oil, or the aesthetic bliss of a well-designed retail space.

Your Instagram fire needs to be as Instagrammable as it is warm. Collaboration with influencers can make this fire visible far beyond your initial circle, illuminating the skies and waters and attracting even those sailing on distant shores.

The Twitter Tribe

Twitter is where the fire becomes a rapid, pulsating signal, sending out quick, digestible smoke signals that can be easily read and shared. Your cannabis brand isn't just illuminating its own space; it's contributing to the broader conversation. Quick takes on legislative changes, RTs of medical studies, flash sales signaled by a unique hashtag— these are your smoke signals.

Your Twitter feed is a real-time ticker tape, a news feed, a lightning rod, and a conversation starter all rolled into one.

The Pinterest Pyre

The fire you build in the Pinterest village has a different quality altogether. This fire is a beacon for dreamers and planners—the kind of people who have been pinning 'dream cannabis cafes' or 'ideal cannabis recipes' for years.

Here, your fire serves as a sort of communal vision board. Create pins that serve these aspirational needs, from 'The Ideal Cannabis-Infused Wedding' to 'The Ultimate Guide to Cannabis Home Décor.' You're not just building a fire; you're building a shrine to shared dreams.

LinkedIn's Lighthouse

Finally, we arrive at the village of LinkedIn, where the fire serves as a lighthouse, a marker of a deeply informed, rigorously researched point of view. Long-form articles that dissect market trends, interviews with medical professionals about the therapeutic benefits of cannabis, case studies that outline your sustainability efforts—these are the rays emitted by your LinkedIn lighthouse.

Epilogue

In lighting these five fires, you've not only illuminated your brand; you've become a tribal leader. You've shown that your brand isn't just a name or a logo but a communal space where people can gather for warmth, light, and connection. Each fire you light—whether it's a Facebook fable or a Pinterest pyre—makes your brand's island a little less mysterious and a lot more inviting.

So, who's ready to set sail and light some fires?

Navigating the Fire Pits: The Perils and Prohibitions

Ah, dear voyagers, if only the journey were as simple as stoking the flames and watching the tribes gather. But in our saga, there are snares as well as sparks. After all, the ever-shifting rules and taboos around cannabis and social media present their own treacherous terrain. Unwatched or poorly managed, a fire can quickly become a wildfire, damaging your brand and alienating your followers. Let's tread carefully.

Facebook: Tell, Don't Sell

In the Facebook village, the greatest pitfall is taking your captivating fireside story and turning it into a direct sales pitch for cannabis products. The village rules are clear: no selling of prohibited substances. Your story must not transgress into a marketplace; it must remain a place for sharing and bonding. Remember, it's about the relationships, the legacy, and the lore. Direct promotions or sales pitches can not only put out your fire but also exile you from the village.

Instagram: Algorithms and Shadows

Just as our Instagram fire should be an art piece, remember that even art has boundaries in this digital tribe. Instagram's ever-changing algorithm is like a shifty, unpredictable wind that can suddenly blow your fire's smoke away from the eyes of your villagers, making your brand invisible. What's more, the village elders are vigilant. Any posts that seem too direct in promoting cannabis can be relegated to the shadows —shadowbanned, they call it—limiting your visibility and outreach.

Twitter: Subtlety is the Essence

Twitter's pulsating signal fire can be incredibly powerful, but it requires a tactician's touch. Here, it's less about what you can't do and more about what you should do wisely. Direct cannabis advertising is tricky ground, but news and education? Absolutely. Be vigilant in reading the winds: Use hashtags responsibly and pay attention to your smoke signals. You can comment on the laws and debate the politics, but stay away from medical claims that could catch the ever-watchful eye of the FDA.

Pinterest: Dream, but Ground Your Dreams

In the village of Pinterest, your fire serves as a beacon for dreamers. But here's the paradox: Too much fantasy, without substantiation, could fizzle out the fire. Remember,

Pinterest is a platform for 'ideas,' and while the tribe dreams big, they respect concrete information. Though cannabis-related content isn't entirely taboo, keep it tasteful, appropriate, and—above all—useful. No clickbait, no outrageous claims, just solid advice and tasteful visuals.

LinkedIn: Credibility and Compliance

While the LinkedIn lighthouse might shine brightly, even the most intellectual lights can attract regulators. Any claims about your cannabis products must be substantiated, and advertising must be very carefully managed. LinkedIn tolerates thought leadership, not rule-breaking. Promoting your cannabis brand directly here can not only extinguish your light but also lead to banishment.

The Legend Continues: Mastering the Sacred Fire Dance

Ah, the fires have been lit, but their sacred dance demands delicate choreography— knowing when to stoke the flames, when to add another log, and when to let the embers glow quietly. And remember, each tribe has its own customs, its own rules, and its own unique dance.

Even as you grow into a tribal leader, you must always be an astute student of the fire, ever attentive to the flickering flames and the shifting winds. Know what can ignite your fire, but also be acutely aware of what can quench it.

The labyrinth of cannabis social media branding is intricate but not impossible to navigate. It's about balance and agility; it's about wisdom and whimsy. It's about being bold enough to strike the first match, wise enough to understand the winds, and skilled enough to keep the fire alive.

So, explorers, are you ready for this legendary journey? The fires await your mastery, and the tribes await your leadership. Onward!

1. Facebook

DO:	Comply with Facebook Advertising Policies.
	Share educational content without direct promotion or sales pitches.
	Maintain a community-driven page with regular engagement, providing value without directly selling cannabis.
DO NOT:	Promote the sale or use of cannabis, whether recreational or prescription.

	Run ads even in states or regions where cannabis is legal.
	Directly or indirectly sell cannabis, risking ad campaign shutdown and potential account deletion without notice.
Reference:	Facebook Advertising Policies — https://transparency.fb.com/policies/ad-standards/?source=https%3A%2F%2Fwww.facebook.com%2Fpolicies_center%2Fads

2. Instagram

DO:	Share original content you've created or have legal rights to.
	Engage with the community, promoting education and awareness around cannabis without direct sales tactics.
DO NOT:	Directly advertise or sell marijuana, regardless of state or country.
	Contravene guidelines; Instagram policies typically align with Facebook's.
Reference:	Instagram Community Guidelines Policy on Sale of Marijuana https://www.facebook.com/help/instagram/789164081427334

3. X (Twitter)

DO:	Share cannabis-related news and info content.
	Engage in community conversations without directly advertising products.
DO NOT:	Advertise or promote illegal drugs, recreational drugs, herbal drugs, or related accessories.
	Share content related to drug dispensaries or depict hard drug use.
Reference:	Twitter Ads Policies - Drugs & Drug Paraphernalia Section https://business.twitter.com/en/help/ads-policies/ads-content-policies/drugs-and-drug-paraphernalia.html

4. Pinterest

DO:	Share inspirational content or personal stories related to cannabis.
DO NOT:	Display or promote imagery, sale, or use of illegal or recreational drugs.
	Share content educating about use or legalization of such drugs.
	Share or promote paraphernalia for using, storing, or consuming illegal or recreational drugs.
Reference:	Pinterest Advertising Guidelines https://policy.pinterest.com/en/advertising-guidelines

5. LinkedIn

DO:	Network with professionals in the cannabis industry, sharing news and insights without direct product promotion.
	Engage in groups and conversations related to the cannabis industry, avoiding promotional content.
DO NOT:	Advertise or promote prescription pharmaceuticals, drugs, or related products or services, even if legal in jurisdiction.
	Share content promoting illegal drugs, highs, herbal medicines, psychoactive substances, or aids for passing drug tests.
Reference:	LinkedIn Ads Policy https://www.linkedin.com/legal/ads-policy
Final Note:	Each platform's policies change; consult the latest guidelines and stay informed about legal updates related to cannabis promotion.

Create Content

When it comes to social media, your vibe attracts your tribe.

—Felicia Lin (@felishalin).

The siren song of social media lures in many a cannabis brand. It promises fame, fortune, and a gaggle of followers eager to embrace what you offer. But navigate poorly, and you'll find yourself shipwrecked, lost among algorithms, federal guidelines, and fickle digital currents.

Between Icarus and Odysseus

You see, our tale is that of both Icarus and Odysseus—flying close to the sun with waxen wings while attempting to navigate past the harrowing sea monsters of federal and state regulations. What worked once doesn't guarantee future success. Many an industry helmsman thought they'd cracked the code, gaining followers by the thousands, only to face the dreaded suspension guillotine. A Kafkaesque riddle wrapped in an enigma

Wisdom or Old Wives' Tales?

"Ah, just avoid the cannabis-specific hashtags," they say. "Be subtle with your imagery," counsel the wizards of the cannabis social realm. Yet, as any sailor knows, the sea changes, as do the algorithms and rules. The endgame becomes a guessing affair, a gamble to see if your carefully crafted 'educational' post falls into the safe harbor or drifts into the stormy seas of deplatforming.

Brands That Row With the Current

Weed for Black Women: A Beacon Amidst Fog

Weed for Black Women isn't just another brand; it's a lighthouse. Like a seasoned mariner, it beams a strong, unwavering light in the foggy waters of Instagram and

Twitter. It's found its North Star in quality, educational content that serves as a compass for its audience. Yet the ocean's temperament spared them not; they too faced the trials of Instagram's ever-changing mood. But they rowed on, prioritizing meaningful dialogue over mere digital decibels.

Groovy Gravy: Stirring the Pot, the Right Way

In the snowy terrain of Denver, Groovy Gravy has stirred an eclectic brew. It has spiced up the pot not just with cannabis but with unique food and cultural pairings. They're painting on a wider canvas, crafting a narrative that goes beyond leaf and THC to include taste, sophistication, and cultural dialogue. It's about transforming perception, one curated experience at a time.

The Dancer Turned Botanist: Julianna Carella

Imagine transitioning from San Francisco's dance floors to the burgeoning fields of cannabis wellness. Julianna Carella did just that, and her brands, Auntie Dolores and Treatibles, dance elegantly between quality and market understanding. On social stages like Facebook, Twitter, and Instagram, she waltzes through with authenticity, her genuine backstory her most alluring choreography.

Marley Natural: Crafting Myths and Legends

This isn't merely a brand; it's a saga. They understand that while Bob Marley is their hero, their story can't merely rest on laurels. Each jar they offer is as intricate as a Greek urn, telling tales of quality and commitment. They aren't just playing the lyre; they're composing an epic, one post at a time.

The moral of the story

In an industry at a crossroads, brands like Marley Natural and Weed for Black Women have not only found their voice but have also set forth a map for others. Navigating the sea of cannabis social media marketing isn't about avoiding the storm; it's about becoming such a masterful sailor that you can cross any sea, no matter how tempestuous.

Navigating social media as a cannabis brand isn't just a marketing strategy; it's an odyssey. A quest that demands both courage and cunning. The brands that will win aren't just the ones who have the best products or the flashiest logos, but the ones who can tell an authentic story while deftly steering through the ever-shifting tides of regulation and public perception.

Don't let complacency guide your steps. Facebook, Instagram, and Twitter? These are the busy marketplaces and bustling town squares. But what about the intimate gatherings—the salons and speakeasies where real conversations happen? Imagine podcasts that captivate with storytelling, SMS campaigns that extend a personal touch, and email newsletters that aren't just skimmed but savored. And yes, why not an in-house production studio to breathe life into your own narratives?

These platforms are your untamed lands, waiting to be cultivated. They invite a depth of engagement not easily found on the usual social giants. It's not just about getting the word out; it's about starting a dialogue that turns bystanders into loyal participants in your brand's unfolding saga.

The time is now. Take the helm, brave navigator, and may your content creation journey be as legendary as the tales of old. Onward.

Strategy	Description
Blogs: Beyond Words	A blog becomes a bridge for cannabis brands to engage curious audiences. Brands like Marley Natural use SEO-optimized content to provide clarity and authenticity to the narrative.
Video Content:	Leverage the growing demand for video content in 2021. Brands can create educational snippets and product reviews to demystify cannabis and foster trust.
Podcasts:	Utilize podcasts for a personal touch. Share stories or host industry experts to offer listeners an intimate view of the cannabis world, fostering deeper connections.
SMS Marketing:	Capitalize on SMS marketing's high open rate and growing preference. Utilize it for updates and mobile coupons, considering the rising mobile internet usage.
Email Marketing:	Craft tailored emails for personalized brand experiences. Diversify beyond social platforms to own digital communication. Leverage cannabis-friendly email platforms.

Master Your Mix

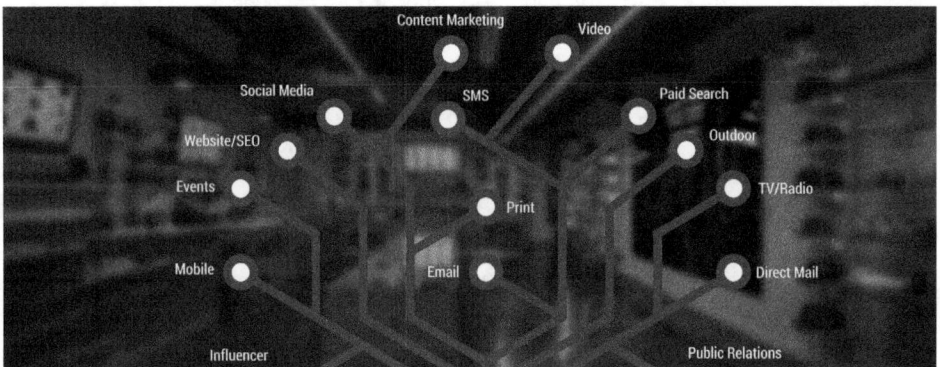

The Culinary Craft of Cannabis Marketing: The Delicate Symphony That Keeps Them Coming Back

Setting the Stage

Imagine a top chef, Laurent, in a glass-encased kitchen where every slice, sauté, and simmer is on display. He knows that the first sip of the aperitif tells his guests what to expect: mystery, delight, and perhaps a dash of audacity. Just like Laurent, cannabis marketers must deliver that first sip—that initial brand message—with incredible care. Why? Because both are artists in fields where one wrong step can turn a masterpiece into a mishap. It's not just about what's on the plate or in the product; it's about orchestrating a symphony of experiences that keep patrons coming back. Laurent does this with a blend of vintage liqueurs; you might do it with a tweet that speaks volumes, a podcast episode that enlightens, or an Instagram story that captivates.

The Channel Symphony

Now Laurent serves an amuse-bouche—a single, complex bite. It's a marriage of flavors so surprising yet perfect that guests can't help but want more. You, the cannabis marketer, have Facebook, Instagram, and Twitter. They're your bread and butter, sure. But have you considered the power of SMS for flash sales or the in-depth storytelling that a podcast series about cannabis culture and ethics allows? Don't get stuck on bread and butter when you could be composing a full symphony of channels.

Creativity Within Constraints

Laurent's soup course is a spectacle. He delivers a bowl with a few stunning ingredients and then pours a delicate broth over them from a hand-crafted ceramic pitcher. The hot broth transforms the dish right before the guests' eyes, blending colors and aromas. Your constraints? Regulatory guidelines on cannabis marketing Like Laurent's ingredients, they seem limiting but can be transformative. For example, educational content about cannabis can be your pitcher of broth, subtly transforming the product-focused posts into a meaningful experience that enriches the consumer's life.

A Complete Experience

For the main course, Laurent serves not just a steak but an experience: A Wagyu beef slice marinated to perfection, lying on a bed of hand-foraged mushrooms and seasonal vegetables. Like Laurent, you can't just market a cannabis product; you need to offer a lifestyle, a transformation, and a journey. Take "Weed for Black Women," which is more than a cannabis brand; it's a movement, a cause, and a community. It's your Wagyu beef experience in a world full of fast-food options.

Mastering the Details

Before dessert, a cheese course arrives. It seems simple, but each cheese is an artisanal masterpiece, months or years in the making. For you, the details could be custom hashtags that resonate with your community or meticulously designed packaging that makes your products collectible. Like the aged cheese, these elements take time but elevate the entire experience.

The Lasting Impression

Laurent serves a dessert that's both a sweet climax to the meal and an intricate piece of art. Your dessert? The emotional resonance of your brand story, summed up in a memorable hashtag, a poignant tweet, or a newsletter that your community can't wait to read It's the part they remember, savor, and yearn to experience again.

The Importance of Review

Finally, Laurent joins his guests for a toast, but his mind is already reviewing, tweaking, and planning. Your equivalent is the ongoing dive into analytics, customer feedback, and market trends. That's your toast to the future, your commitment to an ever-changing, ever-improving feast for the senses.

Your Brand

Laurent isn't just selling a meal; he's selling an experience that will have patrons reserving their next table before the night is over. The cannabis entrepreneur must aim for the same: not a one-off transaction but a lifelong patronage. It's not about the steak; it's about the seasoning, the side dishes, and the sequencing. It's not about the cannabis; it's about the symphony. And just as a chef spends years mastering his craft, you too must continually refine your blend of ingredients in this complex mix called cannabis marketing. It's a relentless pursuit, but one that turns first-time customers into lifelong patrons again and again.

Marketing Strategy	Description
Website/SEO	- Mobile-responsive design - Keyword optimization - Regularly updated content - Internal and external link-building - User-friendly navigation - Google Analytics integration
Social Media	- Platform selection (Facebook, Instagram, Twitter, etc.) - Posting schedule - Engagement strategy (comments, messages) - Brand consistency across platforms - Monitoring and analytics
Email	- List segmentation - Template design - Content calendar - Open and click-through rate tracking - GDPR compliance
Content Marketing	- Blog posting schedule - Guest posting opportunities - E-books or whitepapers - Infographics and visuals
Paid Search	- Keyword research - Budget allocation - Ad copywriting - Performance tracking
Video	- Content creation (tutorials, product demos, etc.) - Video SEO - Distribution (YouTube, social platforms) - Analytics
Mobile	- Mobile-optimized website< - App development (if applicable) - Push notifications strategy
Affiliate	- Partner selection - Commission structure - Tracking system

Influencer	- Identify potential influencers - Contract negotiations - Content guidelines - ROI measurement
Display	- Banner design - Target audience - Placement strategy - Analytics
Public Relations	- Press release calendar - Media contact list - Crisis management plan - Coverage tracking
Events	- Event calendar - Promotion strategy - Budgeting - Post-event feedback collection
Direct Mail	- Target audience - Design and copy - Distribution schedule - Response rate tracking
Product Marketing	- Market research - Pricing strategy - Product launch plan - Feedback collection
Referral	- Incentive structure - Tracking mechanism - Promotion strategy
Print	- Design and copy - Distribution channels - ROI measurement
TV/Radio	- Ad design and scripting - Slot selection - ROI measurement
Outdoor	- Billboard locations - Design and messaging - Duration and timing
Social Responsibility	- Identify causes or initiatives - Partnership opportunities - Communication strategy
Guerrilla Marketing	- Creative concept development - Target location/audience - Implementation plan - Impact measurement

Podcast	- Episode planning - Recording equipment - Promotion strategy - Listener analytics
Loyalty	- Program design - Reward structure - Member engagement strategy - Retention tracking
SMS	- Platform selection - Opt-in strategy - Message schedule - Open rate tracking

Automate Everything

"

Automation is not the enemy of jobs. It frees up human beings to do higher-value work.

—Andy Stern

Mastering the Art of Automated Excellence

The Paradox of the Master Chef

Picture Rodrigo, a master chef who rose to culinary fame by turning ordinary dishes into extraordinary experiences His gastronomic touch was his secret sauce. However, Rodrigo felt shackled; the very finesse that defined him was at risk of becoming his own trap. Between the delicate balancing of spices and attending to each guest, Rodrigo was overwhelmed.

That's when Rodrigo's mentor introduced him to the life-changing concept of mise en place: "Everything in its place. He began to automate routine tasks—chopping, peeling, and even stirring—freeing him to elevate his art. Here lies the compelling paradox: Automation doesn't kill art; it frees it.

Cannabis entrepreneurs, you're the Rodrigos of your realm, and automation is your mise en place.

Every Seed a Symphony

Imagine your cannabis farm as a grand orchestra; each plant is a musician, and each growth stage is a movement in a symphony. A flat note anywhere—a lapse in irrigation, an imbalance of nutrients—and your masterpiece falters. Enter automation, the capable conductor coordinating the violins, cellos, and flutes in your cannabis opera. With systems fine-tuning light, moisture, and nutrients, you move from firefighter to maestro.

Quality Control as Your Culinary Signature

Meet Emily, a trailblazing cannabis entrepreneur whose brand is synonymous with quality. Emily quickly learned that excellence wasn't a feature but a standard. One mishap could ruin her hard-won reputation. Much like a culinary genius using a laser thermometer to confirm the perfect sear, Emily adopted automated systems for quality assurance. It's not just about eliminating the bad; it's about perfecting the good. Automation becomes Emily's personal sommelier, ensuring each product is aged to perfection.

The CRM Maitre D'

As your cannabis business scales, those intimate client interactions become unsustainable. It's like Rodrigo is trying to greet every diner while also sautéing their main course. A customer relationship management (CRM) system emerges as your digital concierge. It's not merely sending canned responses but engaging in dialogues shaped by your brand's unique voice. This isn't administration; this is hospitality—automated yet deeply personal.

Wisdom in Numbers

Sophie, a budding cannabis mogul, once faced a nightmare: a sudden demand spike with not enough inventory. It was her "missing saffron" in a crucial recipe. By employing data analytics, she could preempt demand curves, predict consumer behaviors, and even understand seasonality. This isn't just number-crunching; it's like tasting the air to sense an approaching storm, giving you the time to prepare and thrive.

The Culinary Soul in the Machine

Let's be abundantly clear: Automation will never replace the heart of your cannabis venture. That ineffable something—be it your unique strain or your compelling origin story—sets you apart. Yet automation, executed with strategic mastery, liberates your soul to soar. Just as Rodrigo turned mise en place into his secret weapon, allowing him to scale the culinary peaks, so too can you turn automation into your invisible orchestra, harmonizing your business into a seamless, enchanting symphony.

The essence? Automation isn't your adversary; it's your ally. So go ahead and orchestrate your masterpiece.

Your Blueprint for Masterful Automation

When Rodolfo Opened a New Restaurant

Remember Rodrigo, our master chef who discovered the power of mise-en-place? Imagine if he decided to open another restaurant. This time, though, Rodrigo would need to duplicate not just his culinary finesse but also his entire workflow. The sauces must simmer just so, the vegetables must be sliced to a precise thickness, and the atmosphere must be curated to perfection. How? Automation. And this isn't just a story about restaurants; it's your roadmap, cannabis entrepreneurs. Automation isn't a one-off; it's a finely tuned symphony, a living tapestry that must be woven meticulously.

Map, Don't Leap

Hold your horses, maestros. Before penning your musical score—your automation process—do your groundwork. Which activities are the rhythm section of your cannabis business? Identify repetitive tasks, such as order processing, inventory tracking, or client communications. List them out, as a composer would with musical elements. Without a roadmap, automation becomes a cacophony, not a symphony.

Choose the Right Tools

If a violin is the key to a melancholic sonata, your automation tools are the essence of your operational success. Don't opt for the snazziest technology; instead, choose tools that speak your business's language. Do you need an elaborate ERP system or a simple, cloud-based CRM? The instruments you select—whether hardware for cultivation or software for customer management—determine the richness of your symphony.

Pilot Before You Scale

Even the grandest operas have dress rehearsals. Start by automating a single process —maybe it's your customer feedback loop or perhaps the nutrient balancing in your cultivation room. Monitor and measure. Is the quality up to your standards? Are your team members comfortable with the new approach? A pilot allows for fine-tuning, transforming dissonance into harmony.

Team Training

You've heard it said: "A team is only as strong as its weakest link. Your automation software may be state-of-the-art, but if your team can't keep up, it's just an expensive ornament. Train your team not just to 'operate' but to 'understand.' When they grasp the 'why' behind the 'what,' they become conductors in their own right, capable of troubleshooting and even improving the system.

Continuous Iteration

Our world is dynamic; your automation process should be, too. Maybe a new state law demands different labeling, or perhaps a new social platform emerges as a customer favorite. Regularly update your automation tools and methods to reflect these changes. In a sense, your business symphony is a living composition, ever-evolving and never static.

Rodrigo's second restaurant? It was a hit, not in spite of automation but because of it. It freed him to connect, to innovate, and most of all, to be present.

Cannabis entrepreneurs, consider this: Automation isn't about replacing the human touch; it's about amplifying it. It's not about churning out a one-hit wonder but setting the stage for scaling. Master it, and you don't just produce a singular masterpiece; you become the composer of your ongoing, evolving, captivating cannabis saga.

Onward, maestros, to your next composition!

Step	Action	Examples & Details
1	Articulate Specific Goals	Determine pain points, such as compliance management.
2	Deep-Dive Process Audit	Examine areas, like manual irrigation in cultivation, for automation opportunities.
3	Rank Automation Areas	Prioritize systems like **Biotrack** or **LeafLogix** for seed-to-sale tracking.
4	Choose Apt Automation Tools	For cultivation, consider **Growtronix** or **Agrify**. For CRM, look into **Trellis**.
5	Stay Compliant Always	Use compliance platforms like **Simplifya** to ensure legality.
6	Engage Your Team	Demonstrate benefits, e.g., of sensor-driven irrigation, to cultivators.
7	Offer Holistic Training	For an automated POS system, e.g., **Green Bits**, provide scenario-based training.
8	Phase-Wise Rollout	Deploy systems, like **Motorleaf**, in phases for testing.
9	Regular Monitoring	For platforms like **Headset.io**, ensure insights are being effectively utilized.
10	Iterative Refinement	Refine sales processes based on insights from tools like **Cannabiz Media**.
11	Encourage Feedback Loops	Collect team feedback on platforms, such as **Cova**, and integrate it.
12	Stay Abreast of Innovations	Keep updated with the latest features from tools like the **MJ Platform**.

Diagramming for Automation is a Blueprint for your Success

Automation diagrams play a crucial role in this journey, serving as visual guides to chart the course.

Manage

Begin with visual planning. Imagine it as creating a blueprint for your business. Just as an architect's blueprint ensures everyone's alignment in a construction project, tools that visually outline your business processes, like Nintex Promapp®, offer a comprehensive view of how your operations flow. These visual aids don't merely represent processes; they highlight inefficiencies and areas ripe for automation. By encouraging a team-based approach to refining these processes, diagrams foster a sense of shared responsibility and drive toward collective goals.

Automate

With your operations clearly mapped out, you can more easily identify which processes to automate. Diagrams provide clarity, making evident the operations' flow and potential bottlenecks. If, for instance, a particular stage in your production line consistently slows down due to manual checks, a well-structured diagram will highlight this, marking it as a prime candidate for automation. By simplifying these workflows, you're not only making tasks easier but ensuring a seamless flow, which in turn boosts efficiency.

Optimise

Once you've embarked on the automation journey, you'll find that it generates a wealth of data. This data, when visualized, can be a goldmine of actionable insights. Diagrams can help you interpret these insights, revealing patterns and potential areas for improvement. With this visual feedback loop, you have the tools to continually refine and adapt your operations, ensuring your business remains agile and proactive.

Category	Software/Service
CRM	Microsoft Dynamics 365 for Finance and Operations
	Salesforce
	SAP CRM
	Oracle CRM
	NetSuite
Cloud Storage	Box
	Dropbox

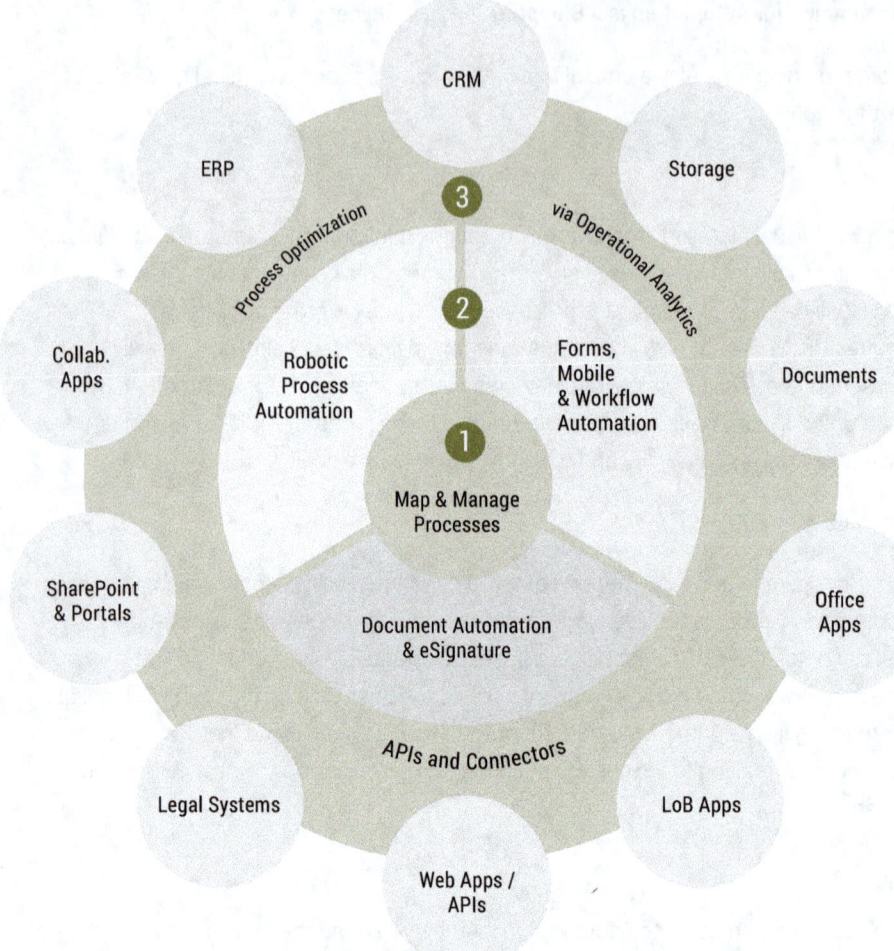

	Google Drive
	Amazon S3
	Microsoft Azure Blob Storage
Documents	Adobe Acrobat
	Microsoft Office Suite
	Google Docs, Sheets, and Slides
	Zoho Docs
Office Apps	Microsoft Office 365
	Google Workspace
	Zoho Workplace

	Salesforce Essentials
LoB Apps	NetSuite
	Twilio
	QuickBooks Online
	Sage Intacct
	SAP Business One
Web Apps	API gateways
	Content management systems (CMS)
	Ecommerce platforms
	Point of sale (POS) systems
Legacy Systems	Enterprise resource planning (ERP) systems
	Customer relationship management (CRM) systems
	Supply chain management (SCM) systems
Sharepoint & Portals	Microsoft Sharepoint
	Oracle Portals
	SAP Portals
	IBM Portals
Collaboration Apps	Slack
	Microsoft Teams
	Google Chat
	Zoom
	Cisco Webex
ERP	SAP ERP
	Oracle ERP
	Microsoft Dynamics 365 Business Central
	NetSuite
	Sage Intacct

Automation success in the cannabis industry isn't just about using the latest tech tools. It hinges on having clear goals, understanding the unique challenges of the industry, and continually refining the process based on feedback and results. Using diagrams can be especially useful in this industry. They not only provide a visual tool for understanding processes but also act as a guide, ensuring every step aligns with industry standards and best practices.

For a cannabis business owner, starting with a well-defined diagram can be a game changer. It helps you visually pinpoint where automation can bring the most value, where potential bottlenecks might occur, and how to maintain compliance. Such a diagram should illustrate each operational step—from cultivation to sale—and highlight where automation tools can be integrated. It should also leave room for regular reviews, allowing for adjustments as the business grows and the market evolves.

As you embark on your automation journey in the cannabis industry, remember that it's not just about plugging in a tool and hoping for the best. It's about strategic planning, understanding your unique industry needs, and always striving for better efficiency and compliance. Using diagrams as a roadmap to help navigate your priorities and ensure long-term success.

Be Active in Activating

Crafting Cannabis Activations That Stick

Let's take a little detour and imagine you've just walked into the most engaging art exhibit you've ever seen. The art doesn't just sit there; it talks to you, informs you, and turns you from a passerby into a patron. That's activation. It's not about putting art (or cannabis) in a room; it's about changing the room. Let's dive into the subtle art of customer activation in the cannabis industry.

Strategic Social Media Engagement

Ah, Facebook and Instagram, the Colosseums of modern business warfare. Sure, they've got rules that make cannabis advertising a Herculean task. But since when did rules stop an artist—or an entrepreneur—from creating a masterpiece?

Turn limitations into a playground. Consider Charlotte's Web, the David who slew the Goliath of Instagram's regulations. They didn't rant about the restrictions; they embraced them, focusing on educational content and testimonials rather than sales spiels. They became a refuge in a desert of misinformation.

Informative Content

Take a cue from a Sprout Social study that said 79% of consumers engage more with informative content. It's not surprising. In the cannabis space, where myths swirl around like mist, clarity is king. So, don your educator's hat. Teach, don't sell; inform, don't preach. Create content that makes the complicated simple and the mundane magical. Be Gandalf, guiding your Frodos through the confusing world of cannabis.

Navigating Social Media Policies

Let's circle back to Charlotte's Web. They've become the Neil Armstrong of the CBD space, taking small steps that result in giant leaps. How? By understanding that the most powerful messages are often the most subtle. They don't break rules; they dance around them. Their Instagram account isn't a shop; it's a classroom, a community, and a sanctuary. Be the sanctuary your audience is looking for.

Activation isn't about a hard sell; it's a heart sell. It's not yelling; it's whispering into the ears of those yearning to hear what you've got to say. In the cannabis industry, where everyone's shouting, a whisper can sound like a symphony. Charlotte's Web didn't just create customers; it created advocates, believers, and a community. And communities don't just buy; they belong.

Influencer Collaborations

The cannabis sector and traditional advertising channels are often like oil and water—they simply don't mix. This is where the influencer steps in, not as a mere spokesperson but as a co-creator, a fellow artist in your cannabis composition. It's not just about their popularity; it's about symbiosis. Their values must not just mirror but magnify your own.

Take Medterra and Yoga Girl, Rachael Brathen. This was not merely a transaction but a meaningful interaction. Medterra didn't just buy space on her Instagram; they invested in her wellness-focused tribe.

A Mediakix survey tells us 89% of marketers get a comparable or better ROI from influencer marketing than other channels. Tomoson says that for every dollar spent on influencer marketing, there's a $6.50 return. These numbers aren't just data; they are melodies in your business symphony, adding richness to your score.

When you pick an influencer, you're not just picking a face; you're picking a world, an ecosystem. Look beyond the glaring number of followers. Dig into the texture and nuances of their audience. Are they jazz lovers when you're conducting a symphony? Or are they already in tune with your offering, just waiting for the conductor's wand to guide them?

Traditional channels may be the locked doors, but influencers are the open windows, flooding your brand with the sunlight of targeted exposure and credibility. But it's not just about the light; it's about the warmth, the color, and the direction. Influencer collaborations in the cannabis sector are more than transactions; they are partnerships in storytelling, community-building, and value-sharing.

Community Partnerships

The digital world often blinds us. The global market, with its endless choices and boundless reach, lures us into ignoring what's right under our noses—the local community. The yoga studio around the corner, the wellness center up the block, the organic cafe where conversations about more than just the weather happen—these are not just neighbors. They are potential allies in a grand mission to redefine value, community, and commerce.

Building alliances with local businesses is like weaving a tapestry where each thread has its own unique color but contributes to a more significant, vibrant whole. It's not charity; it's strategy. When you partner with, say, a wellness center or an organic cafe, you're not just slapping your brand on their wall. You're diving into an already-established ecosystem that nurtures the values you cherish.

Take the example of Eaze, a cannabis delivery service that joined forces with San Francisco cafes for "CBD coffee mornings. This wasn't just co-marketing; it was co-experiencing. Eaze didn't merely expand its customer base; it deepened its roots in a community of like-minded people.

In a world drowning in data, what truly sticks is emotion. Research tells us that 78% of Americans expect more from companies—they want you to contribute, not just profit. Furthermore, 77% of consumers feel emotionally engaged with brands that step outside the transactional box. So, by forging local alliances, you're not just extending your reach—you're deepening your impact.

Select your allies like you'd select a co-author for your most important paper. They need to not just understand your language but also speak it fluently. The symmetry between your target audience and your brand values is the magical formula that transforms an ordinary partnership into a powerhouse alliance.

Think of your brand as a stream meandering through the landscape of commerce. When you form a local alliance, it's not merely the merging of two streams—it's the creation of a new, more potent river. One with a stronger current, richer resources, and a deeper impact on the landscape. These aren't just partnerships; they're new ecosystems, each adding a layer of authenticity, commitment, and, yes, profitability to your journey.

So look around. Your next great ally could be just a door away. Are you ready to knock?.

Customer Referral Initiatives

Imagine stepping into a room where every person already knows your name—not because they've seen an ad or scrolled past you in their social media feed, but because a friend, a trusted ally in their life, spoke highly of you. This is the room where customer referrals build empires.

Telling your current customers to "please refer us" feels a little flat, doesn't it? Sure, you can throw discounts, complimentary products, or loyalty points their way, but what you're really offering is a chance for them to share something they love. They get to be the hero in a story, introducing something (or someone) valuable to the people they care about.

Referral systems can even transcend individual customers and extend into communities, especially when you're forging alliances with like-minded businesses. Take Eaze's San Francisco success story, for example. By partnering with wellness centers to offer CBD wellness seminars, they achieved a beautiful two-step. Not only did Eaze expand its customer base, but the wellness centers also enriched their offerings, positioning themselves as educational hubs in the community.

What's the big deal about community, you ask? Well, Nielsen has put some numbers to our instinctual preference: 77% of consumers gravitate towards brands that have a positive community impact. It's not just about 'you scratch my back, I scratch yours.' It's about enriching the very fabric of the community where you operate. These aren't just referrals; these are endorsements. These aren't just partnerships; these are symbiotic relationships.

Remember that room I asked you to imagine? Well, every referral turns that room into a hall, and every partnership turns that hall into an arena. What fills this ever-expanding space is not just more customers or more profit; it's more trust, more community, and more goodwill. And just like gravity, the larger it gets, the more it pulls. Are you ready for the pull?

Refer a Friend Programs

In the thick of spreadsheets, A/B tests, and ad campaigns, it's easy to forget the powerful army you already possess: your current customers. Ah yes, these happy campers are not just recipients of your brilliance; they are dormant advocates waiting for the nudge to spread your gospel.

Take the example of MedMen and their "Refer a Friend" program. It's a simple, clean equation: you refer a friend, and both you and your friend get a $10 credit. And just like that, your existing customer transforms into a recruiter and a brand evangelist. What's happening here isn't just a transaction; it's the formation of a micro-community bound by mutual benefit.

Here's where it gets juicy: According to the Wharton School of Business, a customer acquired through a referral is not just another number to add to your monthly targets. No, this customer is 18% more likely to stay with you for the long haul. That's 18% more loyalty, 18% more customer lifetime value, and infinite possibilities for more referrals. You see, a well-designed "Refer a Friend" program isn't just an incentive; it's a loyalty loop.

We've talked about building local alliances and the power of customer referrals. Imagine the fusion of the two. You're not just building a customer base; you're creating an ecosystem. A network where value doesn't just flow in one direction but circulates, benefits everyone, and strengthens the community at large

So, let's take stock. You've got this untapped army of existing customers who can become your best salespeople. You have partnerships that can turn into community cornerstones. And you've got data—oh, so much data—telling you this isn't just a good idea; it's essential.

Thank you for your attention. May you deploy these potent forces wisely in your cannabis ventures and, in so doing, achieve not just profits but meaningful, lasting impact.

Educational Events

The age-old dictum, "Knowledge is power," never goes out of style. Especially when you're in an industry still wrapped in layers of social and legal stigma. How do you cut through the noise? You become the professor and the expert; the podium is yours, and the classroom is filled with your future and current customers.

In the cannabis industry, throwing an educational event is not another line item on your expense sheet; it's an investment. For example, let's unpack Harvest, a high-flying cannabis retailer. They've turned their showrooms into classrooms, bringing in medical experts to hold informational sessions. The result? A 20% uptick in first-time customers within a month of each event. That's not an expense; that's what you call a high-yield investment.

An Eventbrite study shines a light on something fascinating. It says that 80% of attendees are more likely to buy from a brand after attending its live event. You see, when you educate your attendees, you're not just feeding them information; you're feeding trust into the relationship. And trust, as we know, isn't given; it's earned.

We often mistakenly think of ROI (return on investment) in simple economic terms. But what if the "I" in ROI stood for impact"? Educational events are the fertile ground where the seeds of long-term relationships are sown. You're not just a seller anymore; you're a trusted advisor, a knowledge broker.

Here's the secret sauce: Educational events transform one-time transactions into ongoing relationships. You are no longer merely a vendor; you are now a trusted resource. A sage in a world filled with noise. These events are your opportunity to not just make a sale, but to make a meaningful impact.

Educational events are your ticket to more than a sale; they're your pass to building a community around your brand. Thank you for your attention, and may you become a trusted teacher in your field, leading your brand to both profit and profound impact.

SEO-Driven Content Strategy

In the digital wilderness, SEO is your compass, your map, and your guiding star. It's not just about making your website discoverable; it's about creating a pathway that guides individuals actively seeking what you offer right to your doorstep.

Picture Leafly, a premier platform in the cannabis sphere. They didn't just toss a few keywords into their blog posts and hope for the best. No, they made SEO the keystone of their digital strategy. The outcome? A staggering 60% surge in organic traffic year-over-year. They weren't just catching eyes; they were converting searchers into ambassadors for their brand.

BrightEdge and HubSpot deliver the facts we need. More than half—53.3%—of all website traffic spawns from organic search, and 60% of marketers name SEO as their fountain of high-quality leads. Numbers aren't just numbers; they're signposts pointing toward a path of engagement and conversion. Ignore them at your peril.

When you refine your SEO strategy, you're not casting a wide net; you're wielding a spear. You're not just gathering eyeballs; you're capturing hearts and minds. And in the cannabis industry, where legal intricacies and social stigmas add layers of complexity, the right clicks are far more valuable than random clicks. You're attracting a community of seekers, explorers, and ultimately, loyal customers.

A well-executed SEO strategy is not merely a tool in your toolkit; it's the blueprint for your digital destiny. It's the magnetic force pulling in not just clicks but the right kind of engagements, the ones that transform into lasting relationships. In the universe of the cannabis business, SEO isn't a 'nice-to-have.' It's your north star. Thank you for reading, and may your SEO journey lead you to unparalleled heights of discovery and success.

Time-Sensitive Offers

Time. It's the one thing we all have but can never regain once we've spent it. Imagine, then, harnessing this enigma in a way that makes consumers feel like they are gaining something, something they must seize before it slips through their fingers. Welcome to the art of time-sensitive offers.

Consider Medterra, a brand you've likely heard of if you've dabbled in the world of CBD. They didn't just drop a discount; they created a flash sale, a veritable lightning bolt in the retail sky. Their result? A jaw-dropping 35% uptick in first-time customer purchases compared to their average month. They turned time into a non-renewable resource that customers couldn't afford to waste.

Numbers don't lie. RetailMeNot discloses that 66% of consumers make a purchase simply because a discount dangles before them. But let's add another layer, courtesy of OptinMonster: a staggering 60% of people leap into impulse buys when a timer is ticking down. What's at play here is FOMO—fear of missing out. It's not just a buzzword; it's a psychological trigger deeply rooted in our desire not to be left behind.

Time-sensitive offers are more than just a tactic; they're a psychological masterstroke. When the clock is ticking, your offer isn't just a proposal; it's a siren song. In an industry as dynamic and crowded as cannabis, where standing out is often a Herculean task, a well-crafted, time-sensitive offer isn't just a quick win; it's a lasting imprint on the consumer psyche. So the next time you're thinking about how to pull new customers into your orbit, remember: Time waits for no one, but everyone waits for the right time. Thank you for reading, and may your next time-sensitive offer be a turning point in your cannabis odyssey.

Customer Loyalty Programs

Imagine your customers as pieces in a board game. You want to move them not just from start to finish but to keep them looping around time and time again. The hidden trap door that turns this board game into an infinite loop A well-designed loyalty program.

Let's momentarily divert our eyes from the cannabis cosmos to the galaxy of Starbucks. A coffee kingdom it may be, but its wizardry in customer loyalty is universal. The magic spell? Instant gratification. Register, and voila, a free drink! Starbucks, according to Accenture, has loyalty members who spend three times as much as their non-enchanted visitors.

Returning to our turf, Flowhub uncovers that cannabis sanctuaries with loyalty programs are like investment portfolios with compounding interest—up by 20% in transaction value and a 25% surge in purchase frequency. You're not merely making a sale; you're erecting pillars for a temple where your customers worship regularly.

Here's a secret, courtesy of Forrester Research: The gift of immediacy doubles engagement. It's human psychology. We're wired to appreciate the 'now,' making instant rewards the kindling wood of a loyalty program's fire.

As you embark on creating or refining your loyalty program, remember that you're not just handing out rewards; you're weaving an emotional tapestry that keeps customers returning over and over again. They become not just patrons but prophets and evangelists for your brand in a highly competitive cannabis marketplace. So, light up the loyalty program torch and illuminate the path for your customers that not just beckons them in but entices them to stay.

Geo-Specific Digital Campaigns

You might have the best cannabis products on the market. You might even have a flair for digital advertising that would make Don Draper jealous. But if you're broadcasting your messages into the ether, ignoring the where, you're missing half the equation. Enter the magic of geo-targeting.

Let's journey briefly outside the cannabis sphere and take a page from Domino's Pizza. No, they're not offering cannabis-infused toppings, but they've mastered the art of location-based notifications. By sending push alerts to hungry souls within a one-mile radius, they've cooked up a 12% boost in click-through rates, according to Localytics.

GeoMarketing tells us a compelling story: 71% of consumers feel magnetically pulled toward location-tailored ads. Even more, these hyper-focused ads ratchet up campaign efficiency by a staggering 20%. Why? Because when messages arrive, whispering, "Hey, we're just around the corner," they become irresistible.

Now, there's more to this. 'Think with Google' found that these localized virtual nudges led to a 35% surge in physical store visits. Ads turn into footsteps, clicks become knocks on your door, and suddenly, digital isn't just digital anymore. It's as real as the cash register ringing up another sale.

Geo-specific campaigns aren't just a tool in your marketing utility belt; they're the Swiss Army knife you didn't know you needed. This isn't mere buzzword bingo. It's a methodology backed by data and proven in practice. By focusing your artillery of digital ads on receptive locales, you're not just casting a wide net—you're spearfishing. You're hitting the target, and that target has a wallet ready to open for your products. Navigate wisely!

Earned Media and PR

You can make all the noise you want about your brand. But when someone else picks up the megaphone to sing your praises, that's when people really start to listen. This isn't just visibility; this is earned credibility. It's your brand's story, but now a chorus of voices is joining in.

Let's hop industries for a second to examine Warby Parker. They're not rolling out cannabis, but they did roll out a spectacle (pun intended) of how a single GQ feature can turn into gold. Their year-one sales goals? Met in a mere three weeks. Think about it: one article, endless ripple effects. That's the kinetic power of earned media.

Elon Musk's Tesla doesn't buy ads; it makes news. The Model 3 launch didn't need a media budget—it became the media. An estimated $48 million in earned media translated to 276,000 pre-orders in just 72 hours. They have no advertising budget, yet they're the talk of the town. That's earned media doing its gravitational pull.

A staggering 61% of us put our trust in journalists, according to a 2021 Edelman study. In a world of information overload, people seek trusted curators. Earned media often comes via journalism, inheriting its mantle of trust. It appears as though everyone's most reliable friend has just endorsed your brand.

Nielsen makes it crystal clear: 83% of us trust recommendations from friends and family over advertisements. Well-executed PR becomes a surrogate for these trusted voices, serving as a collective recommendation that's loudly amplified.

Let's not forget the digital crumbs that earned media leaves behind. Media mentions usually come with high-quality backlinks. Those backlinks work like SEO magic wands, boosting your visibility in organic search. In a digital ecosystem where over half of all web traffic is organic, according to BrightEdge, that's not a detail; it's a game-changer.

When you win over the media, you're not just making a splash; you're creating waves that keep rolling. Especially in a crowded field like cannabis, this isn't just a nice-to-have. It's your brand's secret weapon for growth. Your story, well told and amplified, isn't just your narrative. It becomes everyone's talking point.

Signature Events for Product Activation

Imagine a night where cannabis meets culinary art or a virtual masterclass on CBD wellness. You're not just hosting an event; you're curating an experience. Signature events aren't a mere sideshow; they're the main act, a focal point that turns your

Campaign Planning Canvas

Campaign Name: Creative Concept:

Start Date: End Date:

Campaign Elements:	Assets Required (Team):	Goal:	Call to Action (CTA)	Target Audience:
	KPIs (Metrics)		Channels:	
Budget (Costs)		ROI (Revenue)		

Note: High-resolution PDF versions of all worksheets and growth canvas templates are available for download at www.coolercollaborative.com.

brand into a verb, into an action. Now let's dissect why this matters more than you might think.

Consider **Red Bull**. They didn't just market an energy drink; they sold you on skydiving, skateboarding, and music festivals. According to Marketing Dive, this wasn't trivial—it turned their brand into a $6 billion narrative. An event is not a one-off; it's a sequence in a larger brand story that keeps unfolding.

A whopping 73% of marketers see strong ROI from event marketing, reports EventMB, and 80% consider it non-negotiable for their business success. We're not talking about just incremental sales; we're talking about a holistic boost that reverberates across your business metrics.

Salesforce uncovers that 88% of marketers fine-tune their future events based on data from past ones. It's a feedback loop, a virtuous cycle where each event becomes smarter, more targeted, and therefore more potent.

Why limit physical space when the virtual world is limitless? The Virtual Events Institute found that 70% of organizers attracted a broader audience online. This isn't an either/or; it's a both/and. Think hybrid to cast a wider net.

A study from the Event Marketing Institute showed that 74% of attendees walked away with a glow, a more positive perception of the brand, leading to a greater likelihood of purchase. Your brand becomes not just a product but an experience that lingers.

Eventbrite hits us with this: 69% of millennials experience FOMO when they miss an event that their peers attend. Events become social currency, a badge of 'I was there,' exponentially amplified by every attendee.

Finally, Cvent points out that 81% of event-goers feel more connected to the brand and its community post-event. This isn't customer retention; this is community building.

In a crowded space like cannabis, you're not just competing for attention; you're vying for hearts and minds. Your signature events are not merely gatherings; they're epicenters of brand activation. They not only spotlight your products but also collect data, elevate immediate sales, and nurture enduring loyalty. Signature events don't just add to your brand; they multiply its essence.

The Campaign Canvas

In the ever-shifting sands of the cannabis sector, you need something that's both your anchor and your compass. Enter the **Campaign Canvas**—your foundational framework that's as adaptable as you need it to be. It's not just a tool; it's your marketing playbook, adaptable to the unique objectives and challenges that the cannabis industry offers.

The beauty lies in its duality. Some components are ready for rapid deployment, like a fast break in a basketball game, allowing you to pivot and allocate resources to other critical aspects of your enterprise. Yet we're not blind to the complexities—these strategies often demand a nuanced dance around customer psychology, industry fluxes, and a labyrinth of legal frameworks. This canvas is both your quick sketch pad and your detailed blueprint.

Whether you're in the business of evangelizing new customers, enriching the knowledge of your current tribe, or building a community that's more like a movement than a market, the **Campaign Canvas** is versatile enough to capture the essence of your varied objectives.

What sets you up for success isn't just hitting business metrics but making them resonate. The **Campaign Canvas** doesn't just equip you to hit targets; it enables you to build bridges, to forge relationships that matter.

In the end, the **Campaign Canvas** isn't just a planning tool; it's a storytelling device. You're not just executing campaigns; you're painting a narrative, stroke by stroke, blending business goals with human connections. In the kaleidoscopic cannabis landscape, your **Campaign Canvas** isn't just a nice-to-have; it's your must-have navigational chart for crafting a marketing masterpiece.

Befriend Exposure

The cannabis industry is a tapestry still being woven, a story still in its first act. For entrepreneurs in this burgeoning space, getting lost in the maze is all too easy. But here's a hint: media and thought leadership aren't just your guides; they're your cartographers and your storytellers. This isn't merely about disseminating information —it's about shaping the very fabric of public opinion, attracting capital, and asserting ethical leadership. Let's dive into how these two indispensable factors can chart your course in an industry yearning for direction.

If you're navigating the world of cannabis entrepreneurship, hear this: the media isn't your sidekick; it's your co-pilot. The media landscape today doesn't just inform—it shapes narratives, sways legislation, and, yes, it can dissolve long-standing stigmas. In a 2019 Gallup poll, 66% of Americans supported cannabis legalization, a skyrocket from just 12% in the 1960s. Media storytelling—backed by evidence, not merely emotion—has been a key player in this seismic shift.

Let's consider this: media coverage isn't just about changing minds; it's about opening wallets. A 2021 Meltwater study showed that businesses bathed in positive media light saw investor interest swell by 70%. In an industry like cannabis, where research, development, and scale hinge on capital, these numbers are more than stats; they're your oxygen.

Thought Leadership

Let's pivot to thought leadership. This isn't just about being smart; it's about being strategically smart. It's not just a label; it's a responsibility, especially in a fledgling field like cannabis, where trust is as valuable as any commodity.

Take Neil Patel, a digital marketing sage. His arsenal isn't just information; it's inspiration. Drawing a massive 4.4 million monthly visitors in 2021, he's shown that well-articulated wisdom isn't just consumed; it's revered.

Imagine curating compelling articles, dissecting complex cannabis laws, highlighting product quality, or grappling with the industry's unique social justice nuances. You don't just educate; you become a compass, a trusted guide in an industry still carving its identity.

Thought leadership doesn't just have ROI; it is ROI. A 2021 Edelman Trust Barometer reports that experts and CEOs command trust levels of 68% and 65%, respectively, among consumers. Trust isn't just a good thing to have; it's your invisible capital, especially in a still-emerging field like cannabis.

Consider this: 55% of decision-makers, as per a LinkedIn and Edelman study, use thought leadership as a decisive factor when choosing partners. In a cannabis market that's increasingly resembling a crowded bazaar, this could be your beacon and your differentiator.

In an industry that's still sketching its outlines, your involvement in media and thought leadership doesn't just fill in the gaps; it creates the canvas upon which the cannabis future will be painted. This isn't merely a tactical maneuver for individual gain. It's a strategic imperative for collective growth. By embracing media and thought leadership, you don't just navigate the maze; you redraw it, shaping not just your enterprise but an industry and societal narrative that's ripe for transformation. So, pilot your ship wisely; the course you set may become the map for those who follow.

The Press Release

There's an art to being heard, especially in a bustling, booming industry like cannabis. This isn't your average garden-variety sector; it's a fast-paced world where perception doesn't just influence your brand—it shapes it. While Instagram posts and TikTok videos have their moments, it's the humble press release that often plays the role of the maestro, quietly conducting the narrative around your brand. Not just an announcement, a well-crafted press release is a strategic asset in your orchestra of communications.

The trust factor A 2018 Cision report found that 44% of journalists rate press releases as the most reliable source of company information. Establishing your brand as trustworthy is crucial in an industry like cannabis, where there is frequently misinformation and strict regulation.

Trust is your currency, and journalists are your exchange agents. When almost half of them consider your press release the gold standard of reliability, you don't just inform—you build a vault of trustworthiness in a landscape fraught with skepticism.

Curaleaf's Strategic Announcement Consider the 2019 acquisition announcement by Curaleaf Holdings. By publicly disclosing their $875 million purchase of Cura Partners, they not only dominated news cycles but also saw significant gains in stock performance. This underlines how a well-timed and executed press release can be a powerful lever in your business strategy.

You might think a press release is just for the press. You'd be wrong. As Curaleaf has shown, it is a multidimensional chess move that can affect stock performance, stakeholder sentiment, and brand perception.

Industry Impact Make no mistake—these public statements can set industry trends. Curaleaf's announcement didn't just benefit them; it impacted investor sentiment toward the entire cannabis sector and opened doors for future mergers and acquisitions.

When you lift the curtain with a strategically framed press release, you're not just stepping into the spotlight—you're lighting up the stage for others in your industry to follow suit.

Third-party validation for the win When information has received third-party validation, trustworthiness frequently increases. According to the Content Marketing Institute, 81% of business buyers trust third-party information over vendor-provided data. Publishing your press releases through reputable outlets naturally boosts their efficacy and reach.

In a world of incessant noise, getting an external thumbs-up isn't just useful—it's essential. Your press release gains gravitas when it flows through trusted channels, giving you a competitive edge.

A finely crafted press release isn't just an announcement; it's a strategic asset. Whether you're unveiling a new product or celebrating a significant milestone, the press release stands as a cornerstone in your PR arsenal. The case of Curaleaf demonstrates the broad-ranging effects—financial and reputational—that a single, well-executed release can have. As a cannabis business owner, leveraging this tool wisely can offer you a significant advantage in an increasingly competitive landscape.

So, what are you waiting for? Your story is not just your story; it's the opening note in a larger symphony. Master the art of the press release, and you're not just a player; you're a conductor in the complex orchestra of public perception and market dynamics.

Remember, the world is eager for your melody; make sure it's one they won't forget. With the right press release, you're not just hitting notes; you're creating harmony in an industry that sorely needs it.

Crisis Management

Be Prepared: A crisis management plan should outline protocols for a range of potential issues—be they product recalls, regulatory changes, or negative publicity.

Value Transparency: Open, honest communication with stakeholders is crucial to maintaining trust during turbulent times.

Act quickly: A timely response can mean the difference between a minor incident and a major catastrophe.

Follow the Law: Compliance isn't a choice but a requirement, especially in a sector as regulated as cannabis.

Post-Mortem Learning: After navigating a crisis, perform an internal audit to extract valuable lessons for future risk mitigation.

In the ever-volatile cannabis industry, crisis management is not a question of "if" but "when. The statistics emphasize its inevitability, while the Tylenol case illustrates how effective crisis management can turn a setback into an opportunity for long-term trust-building. For cannabis business owners, having a structured crisis management plan isn't just smart—it's vital.

In the end, a crisis management plan is about more than just surviving setbacks; it's about turning challenges into inflection points that redefine your business for the better. It's about seeing a crisis not as an endpoint but as a learning curve—a rehearsal for future excellence.

Whether you're a startup CEO or a seasoned player in the cannabis game, one thing is certain: your boat will rock, perhaps more than most given the industry's nascent and volatile nature. The question isn't whether you can avoid the storm, but whether you've prepared well enough to sail through it.

So build your playbook, fine-tune your strategies, and run your drills. In the labyrinth of cannabis entrepreneurship, your crisis management plan is both your map and your compass. It doesn't just help you navigate the maze; it transforms you from a wanderer into a trailblazer. Because the best leaders aren't those who never face a crisis; they're the ones who turn it into a stepping stone for something greater.

Schedule a Discovery

Ready to Unlock Your Brand's Full Potential?

Navigating the ever-evolving cannabis industry can be challenging. That's where Cooler Collaborative can help. We specialize in strategically positioning cannabis brands to not only meet current industry demands but to be future-ready.

Why Choose Cooler Collaborative?

- **Expertise**: Deep-rooted experience in the cannabis industry to guide your brand.
- **Customization**: Tailored marketing solutions that align with your brand's unique needs.
- **Measurable ROI**: Data-driven strategies for real business growth.

Schedule Your Discovery Call Today!

We would love the opportunity to discuss how Cooler Collaborative can specifically help your brand thrive. Whether you're looking to improve your public relations, engage with the community, or refine your online marketing, we offer a comprehensive range of services uniquely tailored for the cannabis sector.

How to Schedule Your Discovery Call

- **By Phone**: Simply dial **407-536-7474**
- **Online**: Visit www.coolercollabive.com

Don't Miss This Opportunity!

Take the first step towards transforming your brand in the cannabis industry. We're eager to learn about your challenges and goals and to explore how we can collaborate for your brand's success.

Schedule Your Discovery Call Now

Conclusion

As we stand at the precipice of the cannabis renaissance, we're confronted with an intricate tapestry that weaves commerce, culture, and cannabis. The journey, delineated through the pages of this volume, has been less about mere business acumen and more about discerning the subtle harmonies of a new frontier.

The crux? Distinctiveness. In this budding industry, merely participating isn't enough; it's about sculpting a unique space in a crowded meadow. The tools for such craftsmanship aren't just intuition or tradition, but the empirical clarity that data affords. It's an era where decisions, informed by data, have the finesse of a maestro's baton, guiding the symphony of market strategies and product innovations.

However, the march of progress brings with it an intricate ballet of challenges and opportunities. As technology's embrace becomes tighter, the cannabis entrepreneur is left to balance the grace of innovation with the pragmatism of operational coherence.

Content in this grand narrative isn't just a chapter but a character. It doesn't merely inform; it converses, turning casual observers into avid proponents of a brand's story.

Beneath these layers, like the quiet strength of a novella's protagonist, stands value—unyielding and resolute. Each strategy, metric, and narrative arc should radiate this essence. It's the unwavering light by which a brand charts its course.

In summation, the cannabis industry isn't just a market; it's an odyssey. Here's to those intrepid souls who, armed with these insights, set forth to etch indelible tales on this green expanse. The narrative is yours for the taking; pen it with flair.